Regent's Park Theatre Ltd presents

A TALE OF
TWO CITIES

a new play by **MATTHEW DUNSTER**
adapted from the novel by **CHARLES DICKENS**

First performance at Regent's Park Open Air Theatre,
London 7 July 2017

COMPANY

Irène/Clémence/Young Woman	**Lydia Bradford**
Road Mender/Attorney General	**Séan Cernow**
Madame Defarge	**Claire-Louise Cordwell**
Lucie Manette	**Marième Diouf**
Dr Manette	**Patrick Driver**
Barsad	**Nabil Elouahabi**
Miss Pross/Stryver	**Lorna Gayle**
Jacques 2/Young Man	**Lewis Griffin**
Sydney Carton	**Nicholas Karimi**
Jerry Cruncher/Monseigneur	**Nicholas Khan**
Jacques 1/Gabelle	**Andrew Koji**
Jarvis Lorry	**Kevork Malikyan**
Seamstress	**Francesca Mills**
Charles Darnay	**Jude Owusu**
Monsieur Defarge	**Tim Samuels**
Little Lucie	**Aliya Ali,**
	Foyinsola Ighodalo,
	Olivea Puci
Irène's Child	**Evie Buxton,**
	Mia Dalley,
	Kaitlyn Kou

Other characters played by members of the Company

CREATIVE TEAM

Director	**Timothy Sheader**
Designer	**Fly Davis**
Movement Director	**Liam Steel**
Lighting Designer	**Lee Curran**
Sound Designer	**Christopher Shutt**
Video Designer	**Douglas O'Connell**
Season Associate Director (Voice & Text)	**Barbara Houseman**
Fight Director	**Kate Waters**
Casting Director	**Polly Jerrold**
Assistant Director	**Nadia Papachronopoulou**
Assistant Fight Director	**Jonathan Holby**
Costume Supervisor	**Sydney Florence**
Props Supervisor	**Lizzie Frankl**
Assistant to the Costume Supervisor	**Anne Aurelie Pillet**
Assistant Props Supervisor	**Kate Dowling**
Production Manager	**Andy Beardmore**
Deputy Production Manager	**Nick Slater**
Company Stage Manager	**Rebecca Austin**
Deputy Stage Manager	**Sarah Lyndon**
Assistant Stage Manager	**Dannii Ryalls**

REGENT'S PARK THEATRE LTD

Established in 1932, the award-winning Regent's Park Open Air Theatre is one of the largest theatres in London. Situated in the beautiful surroundings of a Royal Park, both its stage and auditorium are entirely uncovered.

'Regent's Park Open Air Theatre has been transformed into one of the capital's most exciting spaces.'
The Guardian

Voted London Theatre of the Year at The Stage Awards 2017 and celebrated for its bold and dynamic productions *(Peter Pan, The Seagull, Porgy and Bess, The Crucible, Henry V)*, over 140,000 people visit the theatre each year during the 18-week season.

Timothy Sheader and William Village were appointed Joint Chief Executives in 2007. During their tenure, the theatre's productions of *To Kill a Mockingbird* and *The Sound of Music* won the WhatsOnStage Best Play Revival and Best Musical Revival Awards respectively, *Into the Woods* won the Olivier Award for Best Musical Revival and transferred to the Delacorte Theatre, Central Park, New York in 2012, and *Hello, Dolly!* won the Evening Standard Award for Best Musical alongside a further three Laurence Olivier Awards. 2011's record-breaking production of *Crazy for You* transferred directly to the West End and won the Olivier Awards for Best Musical Revival and Best Costume Design.

The theatre's ambition of reaching new audiences beyond the Park has seen their productions of *Pride and Prejudice, Lord of the Flies* and *To Kill a Mockingbird* tour the UK and Ireland, the latter subsequently transferring to the Barbican for a month-long residency, and their co-production with Chichester Festival Theatre of Michael Morpurgo's *Running Wild* completed a UK tour in 2017.

The 2016 sell-out production of *Jesus Christ Superstar* won the Olivier Award for Best Musical Revival and Evening Standard Award for Best Musical, and the production returns to the Open Air Theatre as part of the 2017 season ahead of a production at the Lyric Opera of Chicago in May 2018.

openairtheatre.com

Timothy Sheader
Artistic Director

William Village
Executive Director

Andy Locke
Commercial Director

Kati Donlon
Administration Assistant and Assistant to the Artistic Director

Richard Dryden
Head Chef

Jack Gavin
Deputy Head of Visitor Services and Estates

Cat Gray
Head of Administration and Assistant to the Executive Director

Olivia Hood
Partnerships and Events Officer

Lawrence Keal
Head of Catering

Marianne Richardson
Head of Partnerships and Events

Morag Shackerley-Bennett
Senior Marketing Officer

Elinor Williams
Head of Visitor Services and Estates

MATTHEW DUNSTER
Adaptation

Matthew is an Olivier-nominated director, a playwright and actor.

Directing For Regent's Park: *The Seagull, A Midsummer Night's Dream.*

Other directing includes: *Hangmen, Liberian Girl* (Royal Court); *Love's Sacrifice* (RSC); *Imogen, Much Ado About Nothing, The Frontline, Troilus and Cressida, Dr Faustus, The Lightning Child* (Shakespeare's Globe); *Love the Sinner* (National Theatre); *The Love Girl and the Innocent, You Can Still Make a Killing* (Southwark Playhouse); *Mametz* (National Theatre Wales); *Before the Party* (Almeida); *A Sacred Flame* (English Touring); *Saturday Night and Sunday Morning* (Royal Exchange Manchester); *Mogadishu* (Royal Exchange Manchester/Lyric Hammersmith).

As a writer his credits include: *Children's Children* (Almeida); *You Can See the Hills* (Royal Exchange Manchester/Young Vic) and his reimagining of Hans Christian Andersen's *The Most Incredible Thing* (Sadler's Wells).

A TALE OF TWO CITIES

A version for the theatre
by Matthew Dunster

A TALE OF TWO CITIES

Adapted from the novel by Charles Dickens

OBERON BOOKS
LONDON

WWW.OBERONBOOKS.COM

First published in 2017 by Oberon Books Ltd
521 Caledonian Road, London N7 9RH
Tel: +44 (0) 20 7607 3637 / Fax: +44 (0) 20 7607 3629
e-mail: info@oberonbooks.com
www.oberonbooks.com

A catalogue record for this book is available from the British
Library.

PB ISBN: 9781786822345
E ISBN: 9781786822352

Cover image by feastcreative.com

Visit www.oberonbooks.com to read more about all our books and
to buy them. You will also find features, author interviews and news
of any author events, and you can sign up for e-newsletters so that
you're always first to hear about our new releases.

For Tim Sheader

Characters	Potential Doubles
LUCIE	CHEMIST
MISS PROSS	STRYVER / PRESIDENT
MADAME DEFARGE	21C WOMAN / ONE
IRÈNE	PROSTITUTE / CLÉMENCE / / YOUNG WOMAN
SEAMSTRESS	18C WOMAN / OFFICER / JUDGE 2
LORRY	VALET / RED CAP
DEFARGE	BAILEY JUDGE
MANETTE	BEADNELL
CRUNCHER	MONSEIGNEUR / PRISON OFFICER 2 / YOUNGER MONSEIGNEUR / FRENCH BORDER GUARD
DARNAY	
CARTON	JUDGE 1
BARSAD	RAGGED MAN / PRISON OFFICER 1 / GAOLER
ROAD MENDER	ATTORNEY GENERAL / MARQUIS
JACQUES 1	GABELLE / UK BORDER POLICE
JACQUES 2	TERNAN / BOY
LITTLE LUCIE	
IRÈNE'S DAUGHTER	

All other parts to be played by the company.

The costumes are 21st Century unless specifically indicated.

Once a character has appeared in 18th Century dress, they remain in it until indicated otherwise.

PART ONE: THE WORLD

Three shipping containers on top of each other.

Somewhere not unlike a port.

Yet not unlike an immigration removal centre.

Yet not unlike a court of law.

Yet not unlike a refugee camp.

There are a group of men, women and children. They are dressed like Europe's poor. There are children. They stand as a group and look at the audience.

Behind them, a screen shows images of the modern world: Our great cities, our wars, our celebrities, our famines, our politicians, our terrorism, our protest movements.

Someone walks to a microphone.

MIC **The Period.**

Someone walks to another microphone.

MIC It was the best of times,
it was the worst of times,
it was the age of wisdom,
it was the age of foolishness,
it was the epoch of belief,
it was the epoch of incredulity,
it was the season of Light,
it was the season of Darkness,
it was the spring of hope,
it was the winter of despair,
we had everything before us,
we had nothing before us.

LORRY walks forward. BEADNELL shows him where to sit.

Someone on a microphone.

MIC	**The Preparation.**
LORRY	What time's the boat to Calais tomorrow?
BEADNELL	If the weather holds – about two in the afternoon.
LORRY	Can you prepare a room for a young woman who might come here any time today? She'll ask for Jarvis Lorry.

A seventeen year old girl walks forward. She is followed by an older woman.

LORRY	Miss Manette.
LUCIE	Hello. And this is Pross.
LORRY	Hello.
BEADNELL	Would you like anything?
LUCIE	No, thank you.
PROSS	No, thank you.
LUCIE	We ate on the road.

BEADNELL leaves. LUCIE nods to PROSS.

PROSS	Are you sure?
LUCIE	Yes.

PROSS leaves.

	I received a letter from the bank that said some new information…?
LORRY	Yes.
LUCIE	About my father – meant I needed to go to Paris, to meet with someone from the bank.
LORRY	And that's me.
LUCIE	So…why can't we talk here – in Dover? Why do we need to go to France?

LORRY	Yes. It's very difficult to start.
LUCIE	Have we met?

A beat.

LORRY	One of our customers – was French. A Doctor.
LUCIE	Not of Beauvais?
LORRY	Yes. He had a great reputation in Paris.
LUCIE	And when was this?
LORRY	Twenty years ago. He married – a British woman. His affairs were entirely in the bank's hands and I was a trustee.
LUCIE	This is my father's story. And two years after his death, when my mother died, it was you, wasn't it, that brought me to Britain?
LORRY	If your father hadn't died – if he'd suddenly disappeared – if he'd had an enemy who'd the sort of influence that could condemn a man to be hidden in a prison –
LUCIE	What are you telling me?
LORRY	When your mother died – I believe of a broken heart – she wanted you, at two years old, to grow to be happy, without a dark cloud of uncertainty where you didn't know whether your father had died soon in prison, or was wasting away there.

A beat.

But –

A beat.

He's been found. He's alive. We can only guess what state he'll be in. But let's hope for the best. He's in Paris. He's been taken to the house of a man who used to work for him. And we're going there. Me – to identify him if I can. You to –

LUCIE   I am going to see his Ghost! It'll be his Ghost – not him!

She goes still.

LORRY   Miss Manette?

No reply.

Lucie?

LUCIE starts to fit. It is violent. He calls out.

Could I have some help please?

BEADNELL returns but is overtaken by PROSS. She shoves LORRY out of the way. She holds LUCIE's shoulders down.

PROSS   Lucie? Lucie, darlin'.

She turns on BEADNELL.

Get some water.

BEADNELL hurries off. PROSS attends to LUCIE, who has opened her eyes.

She turns on LORRY.

Couldn't you tell her what you had to tell her without frightening her to death?

LORRY   She's coming round.

PROSS   No thanks to you. Lucie, you're back. Hello. My darling girl.

LORRY   Lucie, you now know the best and the worst. And you'll be with him very soon. You'll be with your father.

Someone walks to a microphone.

MIC   **Blood.**

A large cask of wine is dropped and breaks open.

Someone walks to another microphone.

MIC   In the Paris suburb of Saint Antoine a large
               cask of wine had been dropped and smashed,
               while getting it out of a cart; the hoops had
               burst, and it lay on the stones just outside the
               door of the wine-shop, shattered like a walnut-
               shell.

People run to the spot.

               All the people within reach had suspended
               their business, or their idleness, to run to the
               spot and drink the wine.

People kneel down, make scoops of their hands, and sip.

They are playful and rough with each other. A few dance around.

Suddenly the movement is pained and slow.

A stillness.

All look to the audience.

               The red wine had stained the ground of the
               narrow street. It had stained many hands,
               many faces, and many naked feet. And one
               tall joker had scrawled upon a wall with muddy
               wine *blood*.

'BLOOD' is scrawled upon a wall by a very tall woman, IRÈNE.
It remains there throughout. IRÈNE leans on the wall by her writing.

               The time was to come, when that too would be
             . spilled on the street, and when the stain of it
               would be red upon many there.

               But for now a cloud settled on Saint Antoine,
               and the darkness of it was heavy.

> Cold shivered at every corner. Sickness passed
> in and out at every doorway. Ignorance looked
> from every window. Want was everywhere.
> Hunger started up from the filthy street, where
> among the refuse there was nothing to eat
> except preparation of dead-dog.

> Cities always find the streets to hide these faces
> – to ignore this pain.

*MADAME DEFARGE appears. She is in full 1775 costume. This is
MADAME DEFARGE. She looks at us. She lifts her heavily ringed
hands and begins to knit.*

> But in the suppressed and hunted air of the
> people, in their eyes of fire, there was yet some
> wild-beast possibility of their turning.

DEFARGE looks up at IRÈNE by the 'BLOOD' marking.

DEFARGE   Irène! What're you doin'?

IRÈNE points to her writing.

IRÈNE   Read!

  She dances.

DEFARGE   D'you wanna be taken to the madhouse?

IRÈNE   Blood!

DEFARGE   Why would you write that in public – in the
               streets?

IRÈNE   When?

DEFARGE   There are other places to write.

IRÈNE leaps in the air and lands in the most extraordinary shape.

She points to her writing.

IRÈNE   Now!

She smiles and then moves swiftly away; dancing, twisting, turning.

Someone walks to another microphone.

MIC   **The Wine-Shop.**

The throng disassemble.

DEFARGE moves towards an abandoned car that is now operating as a make-shift shop. Modern contraband is lined up alongside old, green bottles of red wine.

MADAME DEFARGE is sat on top of the car.

Customers sit around and about.

As DEFARGE passes his wife she puts down her knitting and coughs. He stops, he looks at her, she picks up a toothpick and takes that moment to nod her head towards an area of the shop. DEFARGE looks around and we see two men, DARNAY and GABELLE, sat in the shop drinking wine. GABELLE is in 18C clothing.

JACQUES 1   How goes it, Jacques? Have they swallowed all the spilt wine?

DEFARGE   Every drop, Jacques.

JACQUES 2   What a fuckin' treat, eh, Jacques? All they usually get to taste is black bread and death.

DEFARGE   That's right, Jacques.

MADAME DEFARGE coughs again. DEFARGE looks at her. Again she uses the raising of the toothpick to nod towards something. DEFARGE looks and sees that LORRY and LUCIE are sat drinking in the wine-shop, he addresses the JACQUES.

The room you want to look at – just head across the courtyard and there's a door – but, Jacques you've seen it before so you know.

The JACQUES leave.

LORRY approaches DEFARGE.

LORRY   Excuse me – could I talk to you for a second?

DEFARGE   Yes, monsieur. Are you British?

LORRY   Yes, I am. I think you can help me with
               something.

They move away. Everyone looks.

*They whisper. DEFARGE nods and moves off. LORRY beckons to
LUCIE and they follow.*

*DARNAY and GABELLE stand and head over to MADAME DEFARGE.
DARNAY hands her some money to pay.*

MADAME D   Are you friends of the British man and the girl?

DARNAY   No, madame. Goodbye.

MADAME D   Goodbye.

MADAME DEFARGE knits.

Someone walks to a microphone.

MIC   **The Shoemaker.**

*DEFARGE has led LORRY and LUCIE to the bottom shipping
container.*

The containers seem to be inhabited by a great number of people.

It's not easy to ascertain if those people are alive or dead.

DEFARGE   It's very high – and it's difficult. We'll go slowly.

LORRY   Is he alone?

DEFARGE   Who'd be with him?

LORRY   Is he always alone, then?

DEFARGE   When I first saw him – after they found me –
               they said I had to be discreet……or die.

LORRY   Has he changed?

DEFARGE stops and strikes the wall. He looks at LORRY and LUCIE.

DEFARGE   Fuckin' *changed?*

He turns and carries on climbing.

They pass humans in all conditions. Refuse everywhere.

Again DEFARGE stops and turns to them.

DEFARGE   He's changed. He's lived so long, locked up, that
           if he wasn't locked up here – he'd be terrified –
           tear himself to pieces – or – fuck knows.

LORRY   It's terrible.

DEFARGE   Yeah. And many other terrible things are done
           – *done* – under that sky there, every day. Keep
           movin'.

*They meet the two JACQUES coming the other way. DEFARGE nods
at them.*

DEFARGE   Boys.

The two JACQUES glide by, and go silently down.

LORRY   Have they just been to see him?

DEFARGE   I show him to a chosen few.

LORRY   Is that good?

DEFARGE   I think it's good.

He climbs.

           The sight of him is likely to do good.

LORRY and LUCIE follow.

As they arrive at the highest point LUCIE puts her hand on LORRY's .

LUCIE   I'm scared of seeing him.

LORRY   Be strong. The worst will soon be over.

They reach the top.

DEFARGE stands aside and they see a very thin, white-haired man, sat on a low bench, stooping forward and very busy, making shoes. He wears clothes of 1775, an old canvas frock and loose stockings.

DEFARGE   Hello.

MANETTE   *(Faintly.)* Hello.

DEFARGE   I see you're still hard at work.

MANETTE   Yes.

DEFARGE   You gonna finish that pair of shoes to-day?

MANETTE   I don't know.

DEFARGE   You've a visitor.

MANETTE   What did you say?

DEFARGE   A visitor. Monsieur here. Tell him what kind of shoe it is, and the maker's name.

MANETTE stops working.

MANETTE   It's a ladies shoe. For walking.

DEFARGE   And the maker's name?

MANETTE   One Hundred and Five, North Tower.

DEFARGE   Is that all?

MANETTE   One Hundred and Five, North Tower.

LORRY   Do you have any idea why he was imprisoned?

DEFARGE   No. I'd love to know. But – no – nothin'. I'd like to check out – that – that One hundred and Five, North Tower.

LORRY   His cell?

DEFARGE   What else could it be?

LORRY   Monsieur Manette, you're not a shoemaker by trade?

MANETTE   No. I learnt it here – in the Bastille.

LORRY   This isn't the Bastille. Do you remember
           leaving there?

MANETTE   No.

LORRY   Monsieur Manette – Alexandre Manette – do
           you remember me at all? Do you remember
           this man? He used to work for you.

LUCIE has moved to her father. She crouches down beside him.

MANETTE   What is this?

She puts her two hands to her lips, and kisses them to him.

           Who are you?

He lays his knife down softly. He takes up her hair and looks at it.

           It's the same. How can it be the same? When
           was it?

They are all completely still.

           My wife laid her head on my shoulder, that
           night when I was summoned out – she was
           scared that I was going, but I wasn't.

Pause.

           How was this? My...wife...

He suddenly roars at LUCIE.

           WAS IT YOU?

LORRY and DEFARGE start.

LUCIE   Please, don't come near us, don't speak,
           don't move!

MANETTE   Whose voice was that?

He looks at LUCIE searchingly.

No, you're too young. It can't be. What's your name, gentle angel?

LUCIE   You'll know very soon – and who my mother was, and who my father was, and how I never knew how hard it was for them. But for now just hold my hands.

She takes his hands.

Kiss me.

She kisses his cheek.

MANETTE closes his eyes and seems at total peace.

LORRY has turned away and puts his handkerchief to his eyes.

LUCIE turns to LORRY and DEFARGE.

We have to leave Paris.

LORRY   Is he fit for the journey?

LUCIE   He can't stay in this city.

DEFARGE He's best out of France – for lots of reasons. D'you want me to make the arrangements?

LORRY   I'll do it.

LUCIE   I'll take care of him until it's all sorted.

DEFARGE and LORRY leave and head down through the containers.

I want my voice to remind you of my mother and to make you cry. I want you to touch my hair and I want that to make you cry and help you remember when you were young and free. I want you to hear that I've come to take you to Britain where you can rest and be safe. So cry – cry for all that wasted life.

He is sobbing.

You're my father. And I thank God.

DEFARGE and LORRY have reached the ground.

DEFARGE approaches MADAME DEFARGE.

DEFARGE   They're leaving. They'll need food, wine, hot coffee, blankets.

DEFARGE stops in his tracks.

I doubt he'll leave without the shoemaking tools.

GABELLE appears, unseen by them. He watches them.

LORRY   Have you got papers for him?

DEFARGE   Yeah. They gave 'em me at the Bastille.

M DEFARGE   In an hour I'll bring him and the daughter down – with his shoemaking stuff – you see to the rest.

DEFARGE and LORRY nod and quickly move away.

MADAME DEFARGE knits.

GABELLE watches her for a moment then follows the men.

Music.

Someone walks to a microphone.

MIC   **Five years pass.**

The screen shows images of the modern world. We see American, European and Russian leaders – surrounded by relics of the trappings of power: Monarchs, soldiers in ceremonial uniform, grand palaces, skiing holidays, extravagant dinners etc. We also see images of forced migration, refugee camps etc etc…

The performers are all engaged in 21st Century tasks. Stood in groups waiting to be employed. Trying to make money. Trying to make this environment function or feel more like a home. The kids run around in ill-fitting clothes.

Someone walks to a microphone.

The Bailey.

The world of containers, cars etc is used to create the Old Bailey.

In the public gallery are LUCIE and MANETTE. MANETTE is now immaculately dressed in 18C clothing.

LORRY is sat with the defence lawyers, STRYVER and SIDNEY CARTON. CARTON is in full 18C clothing, including white legal wig. He is laid back to almost horizontal on his chair and has his hands in his pockets and seems to be concentrating on the ceiling.

JERRY CRUNCHER, squeezes into the public gallery. He arrives next to two women; one dressed in 21C clothes, the other in 18C.

CRUNCHER   This the Treason case?

21C WOMAN   The quartering one. He'll be dragged along
on a frame – then half hanged, and then he'll
be taken down and sliced open before his own
face, and then his insides'll be taken out and
burnt while he watches. And then his head'll
be chopped off, and he'll be cut into quarters.
That's the sentence.

CRUNCHER   If he's found Guilty.

18C WOMAN   Oh, they'll find him guilty – he's French.
And he's accused of 'avin' assisted Lewis the
French King in 'is wars against us; spyin'; and
of re-vealin' to the French what forces we were
preparin' to send to Canada and America.

LORRY sees JERRY and waves.

LORRY   Jerry!

Who's that?

CRUNCHER   Mr Lorry, my boss.

CRUNCHER coughs until LORRY notices him and nods.

21C WOMAN   What's *he* got to do with the case?

CRUNCHER   Fuck knows.

18C WOMAN   What have *you* got to do with it, then?

CRUNCHER   No fuckin' idea.

The JUDGE hits his gravel with a hammer.

JUDGE   Bring in the prisoner.

DARNAY is brought in in silence. When he arrives in the dock he looks to LUCIE. She smiles. Everyone looks to her. The court buzzes as though full of flies.

The JUDGE, witnessing this, bangs his hammer again.

Silence. The ATTORNEY GENERAL stands.

ATT GEN   It's my duty to remind the jury, that the prisoner before them, Charles Darnay, though young in years, is old in the treasonable practices which claim the forfeit of his life. We know that Charles Darnay is an assumed name and that the man will not reveal his real identity. He's a spy – working for the French and in support of their alliance with the Americans in the on-going assault and illegitimate claim on His Majesty's Colonies. It is certain the prisoner has continually passed between France and Britain, on secret business of which he can give no honest account. Business that might have remained undiscovered, if Fortune, had not put it into the heart of a man to ferret out its treasonous nature. This man, John Barsad, is an example of the virtue known as love of country.

Time jump.

BARSAD is at the witness stand – he is looking over papers.

BARSAD   Yes, these are the lists I found in the prisoner's lodgings.

The ATTORNEY GENERAL nods to a clerk who takes the papers first to the JUDGE and then to the jury.

ATT GEN   The documents are lists of his Majesty's forces, and of their position and preparation, both by sea and land, and can leave no doubt that the prisoner passed such information to a hostile power. Mr Barsad – do you believe these lists to be in the prisoner's handwriting?

BARSAD   Not as you would easily recognise.

ATT GEN   Explain for the jury –

BARSAD   I often saw the prisoner practise changes to his handwriting.

ATT GEN   And when did you first become aware of these lists?

BARSAD   I started working for him in the month of March in the year 1775 –

ATT GEN   Only weeks before the date of the very first action between British troops and the American Colonists.

The ATTORNEY GENERAL sits.

Buzzing from the public.

STRYVER stands.

STRYVER   Mr Barsad – have you ever been a spy yourself?

BARSAD   No. And it's disgusting that anyone'd suggest that.

STRYVER   How do you make a living?

BARSAD   I own a property.

STRYVER   Where is your property?

BARSAD	I can't remember the exact address. I inherited it.
STRYVER	Who from?
BARSAD	A distant relation.
STRYVER	Mr Barsad, have you ever been in prison?
BARSAD	Of course not.
STRYVER	Never in a debtors' prison?
BARSAD	I don't see what that has to do with it.
STRYVER	How many times?

Beat.

BARSAD	Two or three times.
STRYVER	Not five or six?
BARSAD	Perhaps.
STRYVER	Ever borrow money off the prisoner?
BARSAD	Yes.
STRYVER	Yes. Ever pay him back?
BARSAD	No.
STRYVER	No. You never worked with or for the prisoner – your relationship was one you forced upon him in coaches, inns…and *on boats*.
BARSAD	No.
STRYVER	Are you sure you ever saw the prisoner with these lists?
BARSAD	Certain.
STRYVER	Rubbish. You obtained them from another source. You expected to gain something by holding such evidence. You waited for the

> moment when you could fabricate a story and plant those lists within its narrative.

BARSAD   No.

STRYVER   So you're not in regular government pay and employment, to lay traps?

BARSAD   How dare you? No.

STRYVER   And you're prepared to swear that?

BARSAD   Yes and swear and swear and swear.

STRYVER   So you have no motives but motives of sheer patriotism?

BARSAD   None whatsoever.

A beat.

STRYVER   No further questions my lord.

He sits.

Buzzing from the public.

Time jump.

LUCIE is at the witness stand.

ATT GEN   Miss Manette, look at the prisoner.

LUCIE looks at DARNAY.

Buzzing from the public.

             Have you seen him before?

LUCIE   Yes.

ATT GEN   Where?

LUCIE and DARNAY walk out from their positions at court and stand facing each other.

LUCIE   On board the boat from Calais to London, in November of 1775.

ATT GEN	Did you speak with the prisoner?
LUCIE	Yes.
ATT GEN	Will you share that conversation please?

Everyone is very still and listening intensely.

LUCIE	When he came on board –
JUDGE	Do you mean the prisoner?
LUCIE	Yes, my Lord.
JUDGE	Then say the prisoner.
LUCIE	When the prisoner came on board, he noticed that my father wasn't well. My father was really weak, he was really weak and so I was worried about taking him below deck, out of the fresh air – so I'd kind of – made a bed for him on the deck. Charles – the prisoner – sorry – helped me – he helped me shelter my father from the weather. Well – he did it *for* me. He / said that
ATT GEN	Let me interrupt you for a moment. Had he come on board alone?
LUCIE	No.
ATT GEN	How many were with him?
LUCIE	One. A Frenchman.

GABELLE appears to the other side of DARNAY. DARNAY moves close to him.

ATT GEN	Did they speak together?
LUCIE	They did –
DARNAY	We did it.
GABELLE	We did.

DARNAY hands over some papers.

DARNAY   And there's more to do. More people to find.
                More people to help.

GABELLE quickly glances at the papers then puts them into his jacket.

                Goodbye, Gabelle.

GABELLE   Goodbye, Mar –

DARNAY holds up his hand.

DARNAY   Don't call me that. Never call me that. My name
                is Charles.

GABELLE   Goodbye, Charles.

DARNAY   Be safe.

GABELLE leaves. DARNAY turns to face LUCIE.

LUCIE   The man left the boat – as we were about to
                sail.

ATT GEN   Did you notice if they had any papers with
                them, similar to these lists?

LUCIE   They were looking at some papers. But I don't
                know what they were. And I didn't hear what
                they said.

ATT GEN   Now, to the prisoner's conversation with you –

LUCIE   The prisoner was very open with me – we
                chatted about all sorts of things – and so – as
                he was so kind to my father – I hope –

She burst into tears.

                I won't repay him by doing him harm to-day.

Buzzing from the public.

DARNAY and LUCIE return to their places in the court.

ATT GEN	Miss Manette, if the prisoner doesn't understand that you give evidence which it is your duty to give – he's the only person present who lacks that understanding. Please go on.
LUCIE	He told me that he was travelling on business which might get people he cared for into trouble, and so he was forced to travel under an assumed name. He said the business might take him between France and Britain for a long time to come.
ATT GEN	'He said the business might take him between France and Britain for a long time to come.' Did he say anything about America, Miss Manette?
LUCIE	We spoke about the trouble and he said he thought that Britain had made a wrong – a foolish – decision. That the British often made wrong and foolish decisions.

The JUDGE looks up from his notes and glares at DARNAY.

But it was a kind of joke – we were laughing – he didn't mean anything by it.

Time jump.

TERNAN is now at the witness stand.

ATT GEN	Mr Ternan, look at the prisoner. Have you ever seen him before?
TERNAN	Once. In the coffee room of the Hotel Du Beffroi in Sangatte.
ATT GEN	Sangatte is a French military garrison and dock is it not?
TERNAN	It is.

DARNAY walks down from his place in the dock. He sits.

ATT GEN	And did you observe the prisoner in any special circumstances?
TERNAN	Only that he waited on his own for quite some time and then was joined by someone else.

GABELLE appears.

DARNAY	Gabelle.
GABELLE	Hello, Charles.
TERNAN	The prisoner passed that person some papers –

We see this.

– and then after a few minutes that person left.

GABELLE leaves.

DARNAY returns to the dock.

ATT GEN	Thank you, Mr Ternan.

Buzzing from the public.

CARTON scribbles something on a piece of paper.

STRYVER stands.

CARTON screws up his paper and tosses it to STRYVER.

Silence as he opens it.

STRYVER then stares at DARNAY for some time.

STRYVER	Mr Ternan?

Beat.

TERNAN	Yes?
STRYVER	You're quite sure that it was the prisoner?
TERNAN	I'm quite sure.
STRYVER	Did you ever see anybody who looked like the prisoner?

TERNAN   I don't know what you mean.

STRYVER   Look closely at Mr Carton, my learned friend
              here.

He points to CARTON.

              And then look closely at the prisoner. And then
              again to Mr Carton.

CARTON takes off his wig.

              Do they look alike?

Buzzing from the public.

TERNAN   It's remarkable.

JUDGE   It is remarkable...... However, is the prisoner's
              counsel about to suggest we should now try Mr
              Carton for treason?

STRYVER   No, my Lord, no; but I would ask the witness
              to tell us whether what happened here, may
              have happened before; and would he have
              been so confident if he had seen this illustration
              of his rashness sooner?

Time jump.

STRYVER is addressing the jury.

ATT GEN   The good patriot John Barsad –

Time jump.

STRYVER   The so called 'patriot', John Barsad –

Time jump.

ATT GEN   – bravely posed as a colleague and confidante –

Time jump.

STRYVER   – was a hired spy and traitor, an unblushing
              trafficker in blood.

Time jump.

ATT GEN   The prisoner refuses to reveal the nature of his
                business in France –

Time jump.

STRYVER   There is no evidence that the papers presented
                to you in court were ever in the possession of
                Charles Darnay. Some family affairs in France,
                meant he had to make those trips across the
                Channel – though what those affairs were –
                consideration for others, forbids him to reveal
                – even if it means losing his life.

Time jump.

ATT GEN   You saw that even his friend, Lucie Manette,
                could not tell her story without touching upon
                the truth of his treasonous activities on board
                that boat from France –

Time jump.

STRYVER   It involved no more than the innocent chat that
                is likely to pass between any young man and
                woman thrown together in such a way.

Time jump.

ATT GEN   The government and the people of this country
                must be watchful at this time. Our borders
                and our minds should be free from foreign
                influences and the danger that brings.

Time jump.

STRYVER   It would be a weakness in the government to
                give in to this attempt to seek popularity by
                exploiting the lowest national antipathies and
                fears.

The JUDGE bangs the gravel.

JUDGE   Sit down, Mr Stryver.

STRYVER does so.

The JUDGE addresses the jury.

You have heard the evidence of the Attorney
General on behalf of the state, and I ask you
to consider its clarity and its good sense as you
arrive at a decision about the prisoner's guilt.

He stares into them.

So consider his guilt.

CARLTON suddenly jumps to his feet.

CARLTON   Help that young woman.

*He points to LUCIE who has fallen across her father's chest. She is
violently fitting.*

LORRY jumps up.

LORRY   Jerry!

*LUCIE is passed through the court. LORRY and JERRY help. Her
father follows them.*

The buzzing continues.

The JUDGE bangs the gravel.

JUDGE   Let the jury retire under watch. Light the lamps!

*Light has faded. Various lights are turned on. Camp lights. Car
lights.*

*The public move away; some start to cook, some eat from take away
cartons.*

We watch action both inside and outside the courtroom.

LORRY and JERRY come back into the court.

LORRY   Jerry, if you want to get something to eat, you
can. But, stay nearby. These people are my

friends. They want to help this young man.
We just don't know what the verdict may
be and how we might help. When the jury
come back in, and make sure you come in
immediately.

He hands JERRY some money.

JERRY wanders away and gets some food.

CARTON, holding a carafe of red wine and a glass, approaches LORRY.

CARTON   How's the young woman?

LORRY   Distressed; but her father's looking after her.

CARTON   I'll tell the prisoner.

LORRY looks from DARNAY to CARTON.

LORRY   Your looking like each other - it's astonishing.

CARTON wanders over to DARNAY.

CARTON   Mr Darnay! Miss Manette will be fine. It was
just – the stress of the situation.

DARNAY   I'm sorry I was the cause of it. Could you tell
her that for me?

CARTON   Yes, I could.

He drains the wine glass. And refills it.

I will, if that's what you're asking.

DARNAY   Yes – it is. Thank you.

CARTON   That's a very pretty girl to have crying over
you. How does it feel? Is it worth being tried
for your life?

No reply.

CARTON drains his glass. And refills it.

Do you think I like you?

DARNAY   I haven't asked myself the question.

CARTON   Ask yourself the question.

DARNAY   You've acted as if you do; but I don't think you do.

CARTON   *I* don't think I do.

He moves away then turns back.

CARTON   What do you expect from the jury, Mr Darnay?

DARNAY   The worst.

CARTON   That's the wisest thing to expect.

He drains his glass.

              And the likeliest.

He moves away.

A larger group forms, hiding the court. Everyone is watching, on small TVs, cable TV from all over the world. Different languages are heard on the radio. We hear church bells. Some people face east and pray, as in the distance we hear the call to prayer.

CRUNCHER is among them. They all eat.

CRUNCHER puts on his coat over his head and tries to sleep.

Suddenly they all stop. They all run.

CRUNCHER wakes. He follows the throng but is met by LORRY coming in the opposite direction.

LORRY   Jerry! Jerry!

CRUNCHER   I'm here!

LORRY hands him a folded piece of paper.

LORRY   Acquitted.

The crowd buzz with shock and dismay.

CRUNCHER   Good news – good news for your friends.

LORRY   Jerry, you go and tell them. Mannette and his
               daughter. I'm trusting you.

*JERRY joins the crowd, as everyone moves away until only DARNAY
is left.*

STRYVER appears and walks to DARNAY.

STRYVER   The accusations against you were ludicrous.
               But that didn't mean we were any more likely
               to succeed. We've done well. We've all done
               well.

DARNAY   I owe you my life.

He sees CARTON staggering around wine and carafe in hand.

               You and your friend.

STRYVER   He's the most brilliant of men. He was the
               most brilliant of men.

A beat.

               Good night. Go home.

He leaves and CARTON approaches.

CARTON   Do you feel you belong back on earth yet,
               Darnay?

DARNAY   I feel like I don't know where I am – what the
               time is…but – I do feel like I belong here –

CARTON   With Miss Manette?

DARNAY   Sorry?

CARTON   What I want – what *I* want – is to forget I belong.

A beat.

               She was *very fucking pleased* to get your message,
               when I gave it to her.

DARNAY   I think you've been drinking –

CARTON   Think? You know I've been drinking.

CARTON throws his glass and it smashes.

              You should also know that I care for no one on
              earth and no one on earth cares for me.

A pause.

DARNAY   Thank you for all you've done for me.
              Goodnight.

He leaves.

DARNAY drinks from the carafe.

CARTON   Why should you like a man who looks like
              you? A man who just shows you what you *were*
              – could have been – might have been – should
              have been.

He drinks.

              Would I have been looked at – with that girl's
              eyes – in the way he was?

He laughs.

              Come on just say it……you hate the fucker.

A young girl, a prostitute, approaches.

They catch each other's eye.

She indicates for him to follow her.

              As she moves away he shakes his head and
              drinks.

She stops and looks back at him and indicates again for him to follow.

He looks at her.

She leaves.

He drinks. Then follows her.

Someone approaches a microphone.

MIC **Hundreds of People.**

Music plays from 1780. Piano or string quartet. Simple and calming.

Someone on another mic.

MIC The quiet lodgings of Doctor Manette, were in a quiet street-corner not far from Soho Square. Doctor Manette received patients here and he earned as much as he wanted. On the afternoon of a certain fine Sunday, when four months had carried the trial for treason away from public interest and memory, Mr Jarvis Lorry walked along the sunny street on his way to dine with the Doctor.

LORRY appears in 18C dress.

Mr Lorry had become the Doctor's friend, and the quiet street-corner was the sunny part of his life.

PROSS stands in front of LORRY.

LORRY How are you, Pross?

PROSS Nothing to brag about.

LORRY Is that right?

PROSS I'm very upset about my little girl.

LORRY Why?

PROSS I don't want dozens of people who're nowhere near good enough coming around here looking for her.

LORRY *Do* dozens come?

PROSS Hundreds.

LORRY Is that right?

PROSS	The only man who'd ever've been worthy of Lucie, was my brother Solomon, if he hadn't made a mistake in life.

A pause.

LORRY nods.

LORRY	How are the Doctor and Lucie?
PROSS	Very well – when we're left alone.
LORRY	Can I ask you – and if you don't want to say – that's – does the Doctor – when he's talking to Lucie, ever refer to his shoemaking time?
PROSS	Never.
LORRY	But I saw that he's kept the bench and tools.
PROSS	Well he might not talk about it…
LORRY	But you think he thinks about it?
PROSS	Yes.
LORRY	Do you think he has any idea about how he came to be imprisoned – any thoughts on who was responsible?
PROSS	Lucie thinks he has some idea and that he's terrified of the whole subject. Sometimes, he gets up in the middle of the night, and we'll hear him walking up and down, in his room. Lucie walks with him – until he settles.

Almost as though to illustrate PROSS' story, MANETTE and LUCIE walk down together.

> But he never says a word about what's woken him. They just walk in silence.

LORRY	Here they are!

PROSS fusses over LUCIE.

PROSS   *(To LORRY.)* And pretty soon we'll have
                  hundreds of people.

*Lovely music as PROSS and LUCIE set up a beautiful arrangement
of food on materials available to them on the set. While MANETTE
and LORRY bring on a gazebo.*

They all sit and relax.

The music finishes and we hear sounds of a summer's evening.

DARNAY approaches.

DARNAY   Good evening.

LORRY and MANETTE stand.

MANETTE   Hello / Charles.

LORRY   Good evening / Darnay.

LUCIE   Charles, it's nice to see you. Thank you for
                  coming.

He has moved to LUCIE and takes her hand.

There is an exclamation from PROSS.

DARNAY   Thank you, Lucie.

There is a louder exclamation from PROSS who then begins to twitch.

LORRY   What on earth's wrong with you?

PROSS   I'm having a fit of the jerks. I just need to take
                  myself away and sit on my own for a minute.

She moves away.

The others laugh.

It begins to rain and they all take shelter under the gazebo.

*PROSS re-joins them carrying a tray on which stands a bottle of port
and glasses – she pushes herself in between DARNAY and LUCIE.*

LUCIE   How're you feeling?

PROSS   I'm almost back to normal. Thank you,
               gorgeous girl.

There is a flash of lightning and a rumble of thunder.

CARTON walks in.

LUCIE   Sydney.

*PROSS exclaims loudly and begins to twitch. Everything rattles
around on the tray. LORRY takes it from her.*

LORRY   Another fit of the jerks, Pross?

PROSS   Is it any wonder when there are hundreds of
               people. Hundreds of people.

She moves away.

CARTON   Good evening.

He pours himself a port.

MANETTE   Good evening, Carton. Look at the rain.

There is a flash of lightning.

CARTON   Here comes the storm.

There is a great rumble of thunder.

*CARTON empties his glass and then fills it again. Then puts the
carafe back on the tray.*

LUCIE   Listen! Footsteps.

DARNAY   People rushing in the streets to get shelter.

LUCIE   There's something about where this house sits
               on the street – you can hear the footsteps and
               their echoes.

They listen.

LUCIE   Sometimes, I sit here in the evening – it makes
               me shiver to think about it – I sit here when

it's dark – black……oh, you'll just think……it
doesn't matter.

DARNAY   We want to shiver too – come on, tell us.

LUCIE   The echoes – I feel like they're the – the echoes
                – of all the footsteps that will come, over time,
                into our lives.

CARTON   Then there's an enormous crowd coming into
                our lives one day.

They listen to echoes of hurried footsteps.

DARNAY   Will all these footsteps come into each of our
                lives, or do we share them between us?

CARTON's energy suddenly changes.

CARTON   I take them into mine! I ask no questions and
                there are no conditions.

He looks at LUCIE.

                There is a great crowd bearing down upon us.

Lightning strikes.

                And I see them in the lightning.

Thunder crashes.

                And I hear them. Here they come, fast, fierce,
                and furious!

They all look at him. Shocked by his passion.

Thunder and lightning.

The thunder morphs into 18C French harpsichord music circa 1780's.

Someone walks to a microphone.

MIC   **Monseigneur in Town.**

There are images of 21st Century decadence and waste. The rich, the greedy. Wasted food being destroyed. Dinners at the G8. Royal Weddings. The Bullingdon Club, etc etc.

In front of the modern imagery a masque plays out. We are at the French Court.

Most of the courtiers are dressed in extravagant French clothing of the 18C a few of the women are dressed in expensive, tasteless 21C clothes.

MONSEIGNEUR is being fed by attendants.

Then he stands and parades past other aristocrats and servants, each one he passes is lower in status.

We witness submission, cringing, fawning, servility, abject humiliation.

MONSEIGN   I'm tired of Paris. Let's go.

The tableaux breaks and they all accompany MONSEIGNEUR to the car.

He is helped on to the roof where he sits upon a chair.

The coachman, dressed in 18th Century clothes – sits on the roof with his feet on the bonnet.

The coachman cracks the whip then drives the horses as if he were charging an enemy, with furious recklessness.

The journey along the streets is created:

MONSEIGN   Faster!

People scream before the coach and dive out of its path.

People clutch each other and swoop children out of the way.

The coach suddenly makes a sickening jolt.

There is a loud cry from a number of voices.

The horses rear.

The crowd grab hold of the horse's bridles.

The coachman leaps to the ground.

IRÈNE is there – she picks up a bundle from the feet of the horses.

MONSEIGN   What now?

IRÈNE is howling over the bundle like a wild animal.

A ragged man approaches the carriage.

RAGGED   Pardon, Monseigneur, it's a little kid.

MONSEIGN   Why's she making that noise? Is it her child?

RAGGED   Excuse me, Monseigneur – yes it is.

IRÈNE suddenly gets up from the ground.

IRÈNE   Killed!

She runs at the carriage, then stops, fully extends her arms above her head and stares at the MONSEIGNEUR.

> Dead!

People have closed round, and look at the MONSEIGNEUR.

He takes out his purse.

MONSEIGN   It is extraordinary to me, that you people cannot take care of yourselves and your children. God only knows what injuries my horses could have suffered. Give her that.

He throws down some coins.

IRÈNE   Dead!

DEFARGE arrives. IRÈNE falls on his shoulder and sobs.

Women have gently picked up the bundle.

DEFARGE   Be brave, Irène! She died in a second without any pain. It's better for the poor little thing to die, than to live this fucking life.

MONSEIGN   You – philosopher! What do they call you?

DEFARGE   Defarge.

MONSEIGN   Pick this up, philosopher.

He throws more coins.

Coachman – drive!

He leans back on his seat.

DEFARGE throws a coin at the carriage.

Hold! Hold the horses!

DEFARGE grabs IRÈNE, whispers to her and throws her under the carriage.

Who threw that?

He looks to the spot where DEFARGE had stood. His place has been taken by MADAME DEFARGE, who stares at the MONSEIGNEUR and knits.

If I knew which fucking rat threw that! I'd ride over any one of you – crush you.

He leans back again.

Go on!

The coachman cracks the whip and the horses charge.

Someone approaches a microphone.

MIC   **The Monseigneur in the Country.**

The horses slow down.

On another microphone.

MIC   A beautiful landscape, with the corn bright in it, but not abundant. Patches of poor rye where corn should have been. Patches of poor peas and beans. Patches of poor wheat, which, like the men and women who cultivated it, had a tendency to give up, and wither away.

> There was a small village at the bottom of a hill, upon which the Monseigneur looked, with the air of one who was coming near home.
>
> The village had its one poor street, with its poor brewery, poor tannery, poor tavern, poor stable-yard, poor fountain and all usual poor appointments. It had its poor people too. Its people worked hard and to the end of their lives for the Monseigneur; and yet, all its people were poor.

The people of the village assemble. Some in modern clothes. Some as 18C peasants.

The horses stop.

People of the village look at the carriage. Hats in their hands. Submissive faces.

The MONSEIGNEUR looks at them.

MONSEIGN   You!

He points to the ROAD MENDER.

        Come forward.

The ROAD MENDER does so.

        I passed you on the road!

R MENDER   Monseigneur, I was mending the road. I mend the roads.

MONSEIGN   What were you staring at?

R MENDER   I looked at the woman.

He looks under the carriage.

MONSEIGN   What woman, you pig?

R MENDER   Monseigneur, she swung by the chain of the brake.

MONSEIGN   Who was she? You know every bitch around
                here.

R MENDER   I've never seen her in my life.

The MONSEIGNEUR's dining room is created in another part of the
stage. Servants, in a mix of 18C and 21C costumes, come and help
the MONSEIGNEUR down.

MONSEIGN   Swinging by the chain? She'd be suffocated.

R MENDER   But that was it. It was amazing – she had her
                head hanging over – like this!

He leans back, his head hanging down behind him.

MONSEIGN   What was she like?

R MENDER   She was all covered with dust – long – tall –
                white as a ghost.

Cautiously some of the crowd try to sneak a look under the carriage.

MONSEIGN   So you see a thief hanging under my carriage,
                and don't open your big, fat mouth.

The servants seat the MONSEIGNEUR at a table.

R MENDER   She dived over the hillside, as soon as I looked,
                head first, like you'd dive into the river.

Lavish food and drink is brought to the MONSEIGNEUR's table.

MONSEIGN   *(To the villagers.)* If this stranger turns up
                looking for somewhere to stay – keep hold of
                her.

He eats.

The villagers disperse.

They reveal IRÈNE. She has been hidden amongst them, seated on
the ground. She is white with dust. The ROAD MENDER takes her
hand and pulls her up.

Someone approaches a microphone.

| MIC | **Monsieur Charles from Britain.** |

| GABELLE | Monseigneur, your nephew has arrived. |

| MONSEIGN | Tell him his supper is ready – here and now. |

GABELLE nods to the VALET who exits.

MONSEIGNEUR notices something through the window.

What is that?

| GABELLE | Monseigneur? |

| MONSEIGN | Outside. That. |

GABELLE looks.

| MONSEIGN | Well? |

| GABELLE | It's nothing. Just the trees in the night. |

The VALET enters with DARNAY.

| VALET | The Marquis Evremonde. |

| MONSEIGN | Nephew – welcome. |

DARNAY goes to GABELLE.

| DARNAY | Gabelle, are you well? |

| GABELLE | Yes, thank you, Monsieur Charles. |

| MONSEIGN | YOU WILL ADDRESS HIM AS MARQUIS YOU FUCKING RUNT. |

| GABELLE | I'm sorry, Monseigneur. Forgive me, Marquis. |

A beat.

| DARNAY | And how's your family, my friend? |

GABELLE glances nervously at the MONSEIGNEUR.

| GABELLE | Very well, thank you. |

| MONSEIGN | Please – will you eat? |

DARNAY moves to the table.

DARNAY   Thank you.

He sits. For a while they sit in silence.

MONSEIGN   You've been intending to make this journey for a long time.

DARNAY   I've been detained by various business.

MONSEIGN   So I hear.

The MONSEIGNEUR looks to GABELLE and the VALET.

Fuck off.

They go.

I heard about your imprisonment. I was relieved to hear it didn't result in your death.

DARNAY   I don't think you'd have cared if it had. I think you set me up. If I'd spent enough time here and you'd found the right opportunity – I'm pretty sure I'd be in prison here in France.

MONSEIGN   Yes. I'm not currently in a position to ask for these little aids to the honour of the family. France in all such things is changing for the worse. The King is nervous. Of the mass. He mistakenly thinks that when people come together in their dirt and squalor that they take the shape of a tiger. That they have teeth – that they might attack. Where of course the mass is stupid and servile. It takes the shape of a dumb ox. You beat it and it moves slowly in the direction you want it to. There is no danger in numbers. And if anyone steps away from the mass, holds up their head – well – they should be destroyed. One was killed in the next room for accusing your father of some indelicacy towards his sister.

DARNAY	You and he have made the name Evremonde more hated than any in France.
MONSEIGN	Let us hope so. Fear keeps the dogs obedient to the whip –
DARNAY	You both destroyed everyone who came between you and what you thought you could just take.
MONSEIGN	My twin brother had an extraordinary appetite.
DARNAY	He had a brutal indifference to the lives of the poor. I want no part of him. No part of you as his twin. Nothing. I want no part of France. I want no part of this property. Paid for by taxing the people who work and die to keep it going – taxed until they feel like they've been swallowed up by their own emptiness. This chateau is a ruin of waste, mismanagement, extortion, debt, oppression, hunger and suffering.
MONSEIGN	I rather like it.
DARNAY	My mother's last wish –
MONSEIGN	I know –
DARNAY	Was for me to somehow –
MONSEIGN	I know I know –
DARNAY	Make amends. And I've started to do that –
MONSEIGN	Oh, the Doctor?
DARNAY	Sorry?
MONSEIGN	They say, those boastful British, that it is the refuge of many. You're one refugee. You know another there. A doctor.
DARNAY	How do you know?

MONSEIGN   I know.

The MONSEIGNEUR rings a little bell.

                I know about the doctor. About his freedom.
                I know how you *begin to make amends.*

The VALET comes in.

DARNAY stands and looks at his uncle.

DARNAY   If you do anything more to hurt them –

MONSEIGN   You're tired. Good night. Show my nephew to
                his room.

DARNAY exits with the VALET.

                And burn the little fucker in his bed.

*He makes his way to his own bedroom in one of the higher shipping
containers.*

*As he climbs up and prepares for bed all the villagers come and stand
and look up towards his lighted window.*

The MONSEIGNEUR is unaware of IRÈNE in his room.

IRÈNE grabs him from behind and holds a knife to his throat.

IRÈNE   Not a sound.

She turns the silent MONSEIGNEUR to face her.

She hands him a crumpled paper.

                Read!

MONSEIGN   "Drive him fast to his grave. This, is from
                Jacques."

*IRÈNE puts the knife through the paper and stabs the MONSEIGNEUR
in the heart.*

The ROAD MENDER turns to the other villagers.

R MENDER   She said she'd been sent by a man called
            Jaques. What'll happen to us now?

Someone approaches a microphone.

MIC   A year later.

Someone approaches another microphone.

MIC   **The First Promise.**

DR MANETTE and LUCIE are sat on different parts of the stage.

DARNAY approaches MANETTE, who is now fully restored and energetic.

MANETTE   Charles! You've just missed Sydney Carton,
            he was asking about you and when you last
            called and when you might next be here.

DARNAY   Was he now? Lucie –

MANETTE   She's gone out, but she should be back / soon.

DARNAY   I knew she'd be out, that's why I'm here – to
            speak to you.

Pause.

MANETTE   You want to talk about Lucie?

DARNAY   Yes.

Pause.

            Shall I speak?

MANETTE   Yes, go on.

DARNAY   I think you know what I want to say. But
            you can't really know it – that I love – your
            daughter – with – if ever there was love – then
            I love her – you have loved yourself –

MANETTE holds up his hand.

MANETTE   Not that. Leave that alone. Please.

50

Silence.

Have you spoken to her?

DARNAY   No.

MANETTE   And that is probably out of respect for me.
Thank you.

He offers his hand, but does not meet DARNAY's eyes.

DARNAY   I know how close you and Lucie are. I know
that when she's clinging to you, it's like she,
she as a girl, she as a baby – like they all have
their arms around you. I know that when she
holds you she's holding her mother somehow
too.

MANETTE is sat in silence with his head down.

I would never let you two be separated.

MANETTE   She's everything to me.

Pause.

The doctor takes his hands.

If she ever tells me, that you're what will make
her happy, that she sees her future with you –
I'll give her to you.

DARNAY   Thank you.

A beat.

And there's something else. I feel – that – I
should tell you everything. Something you might
– no – that I'm sure – you'd hold against me.
You know my surname, isn't my name. I want to
tell you what that is, and why I'm in Britain.

MANETTE   Stop!

The doctor puts his hands over his ears.

DARNAY   I want to make up for my father's –

MANETTE   Stop!

MANETTE lays his hands on DARNAY's lips. He moves his hands slowly away and his face is frozen in a frown of dislike and distrust of DARNAY.

DARNAY   Are you all right?

MANETTE   If there was anything for me to hold against the man Lucie loved – I would obliterate it – it would be forgotten – somehow – somehow – for her sake. I don't want to hear anything until I need to. If Lucie – decides – she wants you – then wait and tell me on the morning of your wedding. Do you promise?

DARNAY Of course.

They shake hands.

Someone approaches a microphone.

MIC   **The Second Promise.**

CARTON approaches LUCIE.

He staggers. He coughs.

LUCIE   I worry about your health.

CARTON   I don't live the way I should.

LUCIE   Isn't that......

CARTON   What?

LUCIE   Isn't that sad?

CARTON   Yes.

LUCIE   Then why not change it?

CARTON   It's too late for that. I know it's only going to get worse – I'll just sink further and –

LUCIE   I won't hear that you can't be better – stronger.
             I can see it in you; what you could be.

CARTON   You're wrong. YOU'RE WRONG.

Pause.

             But even though you're wrong. I'll never
             forget that you said that. I love you –

LUCIE   Don't.

CARTON   I love you and if – if – you could've loved me
             – a drunk – a mess – a waste – I know that I'd
             have dragged you down with me. And I would
             have known I was doing it. You'd have made
             me so happy but I would have destroyed it.
             So I'm glad – that you don't have any feelings
             for me.

LUCIE   If I didn't have feelings for you I wouldn't want
             to help you. I want to. So what can we do –
             how can I help?

CARTON   If you'll let me say what I need to, then all you
             can do for me is done. You – are the last good
             dream I've had. I've felt less – degraded –

LUCIE   Don't say you're / degraded

CARTON   Just because you and your father have let
             me spend time in this home – this home that
             you've made. You. Since I've known you
             I've had half-formed thoughts of starting –
             again – afresh –

LUCIE   Do it –

CARTON   To stop being so fucking lazy – so obsessed
             with drink –

LUCIE   Do it –

CARTON   It's a dream – that's all – but I want you to know that you made me at least think like that – that there was hope / that there

LUCIE   There is – just try again.

CARTON   You lit a fire. You lit me up. And I want to be able to carry this with me – this – today – that even in the state I've found myself – even as this piece of shit that stands here – that I could open up my heart to you –

LUCIE   Listen to me! You are so capable – capable of so / much more.

CARTON   I'm sorry, I can see I'm upsetting you. Will you let me believe, when I think back to today, that the last time I opened up my heart – will lie in your heart and will stay there – and will be a secret.

LUCIE   Sydney the secret is yours, not mine; and I promise to respect it.

CARTON   Thank you.

He takes hold of her hands.

              I'll carry that with me until I die.

There are tears in LUCIE's eyes.

              Don't cry – trust me I'm not worth it. Give it an hour or two and I'll be crawling around with the lost – with the dirtiest people I can find. But inside – I'll always be – towards you – what I am now. For you, and for anyone you love, I'll do anything. I want you to know – that there's a man who'd give his life, to keep the people you love safe.

They look at each other for a while.

              Goodbye.

Music.

On the screens visions of 21C torture. Brutal imprisonment by major powers.

Images of hangings. Images of beheadings. Images of rotting bodies.

MADAME DEFARGE sits atop the car knitting.

DEFARGE and the ROAD MENDER are climbing the last few steps up to the top shipping container where some of the JACQUES are waiting for them. Some of the JACQUES are in 18C clothing.

Someone approaches a microphone.

MIC   **Knitting.**

DEFARGE and the ROAD MENDER enter.

DEFARGE   Jacques One, Jacques Two; this is the witness.
                He'll tell you everything. Speak, Jacques!

R MENDER   Where shall I start?

DEFARGE   At the start.

R MENDER   I saw her a year ago. I was leaving my work
                on the road, and the Monseigneur's carriage
                was slowly climbing the hill. She was under
                the carriage holding the chain and her head
                was hanging – like this.

He repeats his performance as to the MONSEIGNEUR earlier.

JACQUES 1   Had you seen this woman before?

R MENDER   Never.

He straightens up.

JACQUES 1   How did you recognise her later then?

R MENDER   She was so tall. When the Monseigneur asked
                me, 'What is she like?' I said, 'Long – tall'.

JACQUES 2   You should have said short as a dwarf.

55

R MENDER   But what did I know? Nothing had happened
            then.

DEFARGE   He's right, Jacques. Go on!

R MENDER   Then she disappeared – for what – ten, eleven
            months?

DEFARGE   We didn't hide her well enough. Somehow
            they found her.

R MENDER   Again I'm working at the same road on the
            hill-side, when I look up and see six soldiers
            with the tall woman in the middle of them.
            Her arms were swollen 'cause they were tied to
            her sides – like this!

He imitates someone with their elbows bound fast to their sides.

            When they get closer, I recognise the tall
            woman and she recognises me. We don't show
            it – to the soldiers. We know it – with our eyes.
            She's limping badly – so the soldiers drive her
            on with their guns – like this!

*He imitates the action of the woman being impelled forward by the
butt-ends of muskets.*

            They make her run down the hill. She falls.
            They laugh. When they pick her up her face is
            bleeding and covered in dust. They bring her
            into the village – all the village runs to look.
            The Sunday before, when everyone was asleep,
            the soldiers, had put a gallows, right by the
            fountain, about forty feet high.

            They put a gag in the tall woman's mouth and
            tie it with a really tight string – like this!

*He imitates by creasing his face with his two thumbs from the corners
of his mouth to his ears.*

> There's a drum roll. And then they hang her
> there – forty feet high – and they left her there
> – hanging – poisoning the water.

Silence – as they all look at each other.

JACQUES 1   Will you wait for us – outside the door?

R MENDER   Yes.

DEFARGE escorts him out, then returns.

JACQUES 1   What do you think, Jacques?

DEFARGE   To be registered under: 'to be destroyed'.

JACQUES 2   But the Monseigneur is already dead.

JACQUES 1   The chateau, and all the family Evremonde.

DEFARGE   The chateau and all the family.

JACQUES 2   Are you sure the way your wife keeps the
register is safe?

DEFARGE   Jacques, if she only kept the register in her
head, she wouldn't lose a word of it. Knitting it
– in her own stitches and her own symbols, it's
as plain to her as the sun.

They all nod.

JACQUES 2   It's good.

JACQUES 1   Is this idiot to be sent back – isn't he
dangerous?

DEFARGE   I'll take care of him, and make sure he sets off
on the right road. He wants to see the finery of
Paris – the King, the Queen, and the Court.

A JACQUES   Is that a good sign, that he wants to see Royalty?

DEFARGE   Show a dog his natural prey,

Then he'll bite its throat one day.

There is an extraordinary fanfare. With it comes a glorious, golden vision of Louis XVI and Marie Antoinette.

The ROAD MENDER is stood in front of the vision in awe.

As the vision disappears, the ROAD MENDER turns out to the audience and spits on the ground in disgust.

The music changes.

MADAME DEFARGE is sat on the car knitting.

Someone approaches a microphone.

MIC   **Still Knitting.**

They part and DEFARGE approaches his wife.

DEFARGE   There is a spy from Britain. Asking questions
             about our quarter – about the Jacques.

MADAME D   From Britain?

DEFARGE   Why would he come here?

MADAME D   All governments of kings have something to
             fear.

DEFARGE   Jacques of the police says he's been asking
             about us.

MADAME D   Why us? Why would he know about us?

DEFARGE   They have a name. Barsad.

She knits.

MADAME D   Barsad. Christian name?

DEFARGE   Erm… John.

MADAME D   Good.

She knits.

He sits and stares into space.

MADAME D   Well we shall see. You're exhausted.

DEFARGE   Yeah.

A beat.

            When I think about what happened to Irène.

MADAME D   There will be vengeance. There will be
            retribution.

DEFARGE   It'll take so much time.

MADAME D   Tell me how long it takes to prepare an
            earthquake.

DEFARGE   A long time.

MADAME D   But when it's ready, it grinds everything that
            stands in its way to pieces. Until then, it's
            always preparing and it isn't seen and it isn't
            heard. That's what should keep you going.

DEFARGE   You know it's possible – that it may not come –
            during our lives. We won't see the victory.

MADAME D   We will have helped it. We just need to always
            be ready. Now go and wash your face. Clear
            your head.

He nods and leaves.

BARSAD enters. He is in 18C clothing.

BARSAD   Good afternoon, Madame.

MADAME D   Good afternoon, Monsieur.

BARSAD   A small glass of cognac and some fresh water,
            please.

*MADAME DEFARGE gets his drinks. She is stern but uses it to flirt
and tease.*

            A nice little shop.

MADAME D   Thank you.

BARSAD	Do you run the place?
MADAME D	Yes.
BARSAD	With your husband?
MADAME D	I have a husband.
BARSAD	Children?
MADAME D	No children.
BARSAD	Business doesn't seem great.
MADAME D	Business is bad; people are so poor.

She is knitting again.

BARSAD	Yeah – so oppressed, too – as you say.
MADAME D	As *you* say.

A beat.

BARSAD	You knit brilliantly.
MADAME D	I've practised a lot.
BARSAD	And that's a nice pattern.
MADAME D	You think so?
BARSAD	Definitely. What's it for?
MADAME D	Just to pass the time.
BARSAD	Not for use?
MADAME D	I might find a use for it one day.

Pause. She knits.

BARSAD	A bad business all that – that young woman's hanging.

He shakes his head.

The poor bitch.

MADAME D   What? If you use a knife – you know the price
            you're gonna pay. She's paid the price.

BARSAD looks around and lowers his voice.

BARSAD   It's always people like Irène that have to pay
            the price though. Isn't it? If you dare to
            stand up to those bastards. He killed her kid.
            He killed her kid. There must be so much
            – anger – and sympathy for Irène – in this
            neighbourhood?

MADAME D   Is there?

BARSAD   Is there not?

A beat. DEFARGE returns.

MADAME D   Here's my husband!

BARSAD   Afternoon, Jacques!

DEFARGE   You must be confusing me with someone else,
            monsieur. I'm Ernest Defarge.

BARSAD   It's all the same.

A beat.

            I was just saying to your wife – that I hear –
            that people around here are really angry about
            what happened to Irène.

DEFARGE   No one's said that to me. But perhaps you
            know this quarter better than I do.

BARSAD   No – I don't think so. But I'm interested –
            in people – and people around here are poor
            and pissed off.

DEFARGE   They're poor. I'll give you that.

A beat.

BARSAD   *(To MADAME DEFARGE.)* I'll have another
               cognac, please.

She goes to get it for him.

               You know – I've heard your name before.

DEFARGE   Really?

BARSAD   Yeah – really. You're Dr Manette's old servant
               aren't you? And when he was released you
               were given custody of him.

DEFARGE   That's all – correct.

BARSAD   His daughter came to you – and took him from
               here – with – what's his name – Lorry – of
               Tellson's bank.

DEFARGE   That's right.

BARSAD   That's all really interesting – to me. I've met
               Doctor Manette and his daughter, in England.

DEFARGE   Yes?

BARSAD   Do you still hear from them?

MADAME D   They let us know they'd arrived home safely.
               And…maybe – another letter or two; but,
               since then, I guess they're making a life for
               themselves in England.

BARSAD   She's about to get married.

MADAME D   She's so pretty I'm surprised she isn't married
               already. You English are cold, I reckon.

BARSAD   You know I'm English?

MADAME D   Your tongue is. So I guess you are.

BARSAD smiles.

*Elsewhere, CHARLES and MANETTE, both in 18C suits ready for a
wedding, shake hands. MANETTE looks terrified.*

BARSAD   Yes, she's going to be married.

DARNAY   I promised that on the morning of the wedding –

BARSAD   But not to a Britishman. He's French.

DARNAY   That I'd tell you my family's name in France.

BARSAD   Charles Darnay.

DARNAY   And why I am in England.

MANETTE   Let's go into my room.

MANETTE and DARNAY move off.

LORRY walks forward and looks after them.

BARSAD   That's not his real name. It's Evremonde.
            He's the nephew of the Monseigneur whose
            murder meant poor old Irène had to swing
            from forty feet. So the man Lucie Manette is
            marrying inherits all that was his.

MADAME DEFARGE knits steadily.

BARSAD hands over some money.

            I need to go. But I look forward to seeing you
            both again.

BARSAD leaves.

DEFARGE   An Evremonde. That family again.

MADAME D   Yes. Again.

DEFARGE   For Manette's daughter's sake – I hope her
            husband never sets foot back in France.

MADAME D   He'll go where his destiny takes him. And if
            it's France – we'll be waiting.

MADAME DEFARGE knits.

Someone approaches a microphone.

MIC **A Morning.**

PROSS hurries forward and joins LORRY.

PROSS   What a day.

LORRY   It's wonderful isn't it?

PROSS   Of course. My darlin' looks so pretty in her dress. He's a very lucky man.

LORRY   He is.

PROSS   But I just think – that if my brother Solomon had been the groom –

LORRY   Oh come on, Pross!

PROSS   Then the day could be even more blissful.

LORRY   But you're happy for them?

PROSS   Of course of course.

LUCIE walks down in an 18C wedding dress.

With my angel looking so perfect.

The women hug.

LORRY   So, Lucie – this is why I brought you across the channel when you were small.

LUCIE   Maybe it was.

PROSS   Don't be ridiculous – you didn't know. How could you know?

DARNAY and MANETTE re-appear.

MANETTE is visibly shaken. CHARLES is alarmed at the affect his revelation has had.

MANETTE holds out his hand to his daughter.

LUCIE   Father, are you OK?

MANETTE   Take her, Charles. She's yours.

Bells ring as LORRY takes a ring from his pocket and hands it to CHARLES.

There is a wedding tableaux.

Bells ring.

They all disperse:

The couple move happily away arm in arm.

PROSS looks after them sobbing and waving.

MANETTE walks slowly away, head bowed.

LORRY sits with a drink. He looks happy and satisfied.

Suddenly there is a knocking sound.

He sits upright.

LORRY   Good God! What's that?

PROSS runs in.

PROSS   It's happening. It's all over. What shall we tell
               the little girl? He doesn't know who I am and
               he's making shoes.

Someone approaches a microphone.

MIC   **A Night.**

They move to another part of the space.

As they discover MANETTE, so do we.

He is at his shoemaking bench working away.

LORRY   Alexandre? Doctor Manette?

MANETTE briefly looks up. Then back to work.

               What are you making?

MANETTE   It's a ladies shoe. For walking. And it
               should've been finished a long time ago.

LORRY   And who are you?

MANETTE   One Hundred and Five, North Tower.

LORRY   No, Doctor Manette, look at me.

MANETTE mechanically looks – but without stopping working.

You know me – we're friends. This is not your
occupation. You're a doctor.

MANETTE turns back to his work.

Will you go out?

MANETTE looks at his surroundings.

MANETTE   Out?

LORRY   Yes, for a walk. You like walking. You love
walking with your daughter, Lucie.

MANETTE   No.

LORRY   Yes. This is Lucie's friend, Pross. Take her arm.

*LORRY gently lifts MANETTE away from his bench and PROSS takes
his arm. She walks with him. Up and down. Up and down.*

LORRY observes them.

Clearly MANETTE becomes more aware of himself as they walk.

Alexandre, I need your opinion on something;
in confidence. It's regarding a very good
friend of mine.

*After a time PROSS stops and backs away and lets MANETTE walk
on his own. Up and down. Up and down. He continues to walk
this pattern as LORRY interviews him.*

And please turn your full attention to it – for
his sake – but mostly for his daughter.

MANETTE   I think I understand. Is it about a – a mental
shock?

LORRY   Yes.

MANETTE   Tell me everything. Don't hide anything or
             feel you need to protect anyone.

LORRY   We thought he'd recovered completely from a
             major shock. But – unfortunately, there's been
             – a slight relapse.

MANETTE stops his walking for a beat. Continues.

MANETTE   How did it show itself?

He looks at his hands.

             Did he go back to – some old activity – connected
             with the shock?

LORRY   Yes.

MANETTE   Did you ever see him when he was originally
             engaged in that activity?

LORRY   Some years ago now – but – yes – once.

MANETTE   And when he relapsed – was his behaviour –
             his state of mind –

LORRY   The same.

MANETTE   Does his daughter know about the relapse?

LORRY   No. Only I know – and one other who we can
             trust.

MANETTE   I think it's probable that the relapse you
             describe was expected by him.

MANETTE stops.

Silence.

DARNAY, in his wedding costume has walked forward.

             And that – if something he *suspected* –

DARNAY turns to MANETTE.

67

DARNAY   My family's name is Evremonde. My father
            and my uncle tried to destroy you.

MANETTE   If something he *suspected* – was *true* – then –
            associations would be recalled – and despite
            the efforts he made to prepare himself – he
            might not able to bear it.

DARNAY moves away and disappears.

LORRY   And is there a best way – to move on – to
            move forward?

MANETTE   I would have – real hope. Especially as this
            time he recovered so soon.

A beat.

LORRY   The work he does, when he is in this state of
            shock – let's say it's Blacksmith's work. He
            needs a forge to work. Is it not a shame that he
            keeps this forge – in his home?

MANETTE starts walking again.

            Would it not be better if he let it go?

MANETTE   It's been a very good friend to him.

LORRY   For his daughter's sake?

MANETTE stops walking.

MANETTE   For his daughter's sake – I agree. But I
            wouldn't take it away when he's around.

MANETTE walks away.

PROSS brings LORRY an axe.

He goes to the table and begins to smash it to pieces.

Someone walks to a microphone.

MIC   **Echoing Footsteps.**

Someone walks to another microphone.

MIC   Lucie Darnay loved living in her corner of
Soho. But whenever she sat in the still, quiet
house, she heard the echoing footsteps of
the years ahead. Something was coming,
something far off, that was scarcely audible,
but that filled her with doubt. But her fears
were held at bay by a new love and hope; as
now there was a little Lucie; now, among the
advancing footsteps, there were the sounds of
tinier feet and prattling words in a mix of the
French and English of the Two Cities that were
blended into Lucie's life.

Six year old LITTLE LUCIE walks forward and is held by her mother.

It was at the time of Little Lucie's sixth
birthday, that the echoes grew louder and
louder until they reached a menacing pitch.

LORRY walks forward.

LORRY   There is such an uneasiness in Paris, our
customers over there cannot transfer their
holdings to London fast enough. When there
is no confidence in a city, money pours out
of it. Lucie, you had your theory about the
footsteps, and there are as many of them as
you said. And they are as loud.

A group of men and women walk towards the audience.

Someone walks to another microphone.

MIC   And there were footsteps, footsteps raging far
away as they march out of Saint Antoine, mad
and dangerous through the Paris streets. And
this time, so long after the breaking of the cask
at Defarge's wine-shop door, these feet will not
be easily cleansed when once more stained red.

Someone walks to another microphone.

MIC   **The Storm**.

Someone walks to another microphone.

MIC   Every pulse and heart in Saint Antoine was on high-fever strain and at high-fever heat. Every living creature there held life as of no account, and was demented with a passionate readiness to sacrifice it. A forest of naked arms clutched at every weapon or semblance of a weapon.

The group of men and women, are in a mix of 18C and 21C clothes. They are passed axes, iron bars, baseball bats, bricks etc. Someone has a musket – someone has a modern hand gun.

People who could lay hold of nothing else, set themselves with bleeding hands to force stones and bricks out of walls.

The DEFARGEs appear.

DEFARGE instructs the assembled JACQUES.

DEFARGE   Keep near to me, Jacques Two. Jacques One, put yourself at the head of as many of these patriots as you can.

JACQUES 1   Now they'll fuckin' listen to us. Now they'll know we're here.

MADAME DEFARGE joins DEFARGE. She has an axe in her hand and a pistol and a knife in her belt.

DEFARGE   What will you do?

M DEFARGE   I'll round up and lead the women.

DEFARGE   Come on then! Friends, patriots – we are ready! The Bastille!

A horrific roar.

Alarm bells ring.

Drums beat.

A modern prison klaxon sounds.

The attack begins.

Gun and canon fire.

Through the smoke the battle is viciously waged.

DEFARGE   Work, comrades, work! Push forward. We
               must break through. Work, Jacques One,
               Jacques Two, Jacques One Thousand, Jacques
               Two Thousand, Jacques Twenty Thousand in /
               the name of God or the Devil – whoever you
               fuckin' prefer – work!

M DEFARGE   Women with me. Push forward 'til the Bastille
               is ours. We can kill as well as the men when
               this bastard place is taken!

   She and her women fight.

MIC   A white flag from within the fortress that is the
               Bastille, dimly perceptible through the raging
               storm of smoke and fire. A surrender. Defarge
               of the wine-shop is swept over the lowered
               drawbridge, past the massive stone outer walls.

DEFARGE   The Prisoners!

M DEFARGE   The Records!

DEFARGE   The secret cells!

JAQUES 1   The instruments of torture!

DEFARGE   The Prisoners!

   DEFARGE grabs a PRISON OFFICER carrying a torch.

               Show me the North Tower. Quick!

P OFFICER   I can – but there's no one there.

DEFARGE	What's the meaning of One Hundred and Five, North Tower? Quick!
P OFFICER	The meaning?
DEFARGE	Does it mean a prisoner or a cell?
A JACQUES	Kill him!
P OFFICER	It's a cell.
DEFARGE	Show it me!
JAQUES 2	Why? There is so much to do.
DEFARGE	I need to see it. I have to look.
P OFFICER	Pass this way, then.

They go up high.

They pass death and murder and chaos.

The PRISON OFFICER opens the door.

P OFFICER	One hundred and five, North Tower.

DEFARGE and A JACQUES search frantically – ripping at everything.

A JACQUES	What are we looking for?
DEFARGE	Dunno – maybe nothing. Pass that torch slowly along these walls, so I can see them.

The PRISON OFFICER does so.

Stop. Look at this Jaques.

There are letters faintly scratched into a wall.

A JACQUES	A.M.
DEFARGE	Alexandre Manette.

DEFARGE opens part of the shipping container. He gropes around with his hand. He pulls out some papers.

DEFARGE	I knew it. I knew we'd find something.

DEFARGE stuffs the papers into his jacket.

Back in the yard everything around is burning.

Drums.

A crowd begin to kick and attack a PRISON OFFICER.

MADAME DEFARGE stands over the PRISON OFFICER.

She takes out the knife from her belt.

DEFARGE sees her.

DEFARGE   Wait!

M DEFARGE   Watch, Defarge. Watch!

Using her knife she hews off the PRISON OFFICER's head.

She holds it up.

A roar from everyone.

            See, Defarge!

Drums.

            See!

Interval.

PART TWO: FROM THE DARKNESS

The environment is the same as Part One, but all costumes and props are 18C, until otherwise specified.

The ROAD MENDER enters.

JACQUES ONE, in a red cap, enters and walks up to him.

Someone walks to a microphone.

MIC	**Fire Rises.**
JACQUES 1	How goes it, Jacques?
R MENDER	All well, Jacques.
JACQUES 1	Touch then.

They join hands.

> No dinner?

R MENDER	No.

A JACQUES shakes his head.

JACQUES 1	I meet no dinner anywhere.

JACQUES ONE takes out a blackened pipe, lights it with flint and steel, pulls at it until it's in a bright glow: then, he holds it from him and drops something into it from between his finger and thumb it blazes and then goes out.

The ROAD MENDER nods.

R MENDER	Tonight?
JACQUES 1	Tonight. Show me.
R MENDER	You go down here to the village, walk down the street, and past the fountain –
JACQUES 1	Where they hung Irène?
R MENDER	Yes – past the fountain and –

JACQUES 1	Bollocks to that. I'm not going down any fuckin' street and past no bastard fountains.
R MENDER	Over that way then. Scoot round that hill above the village.
JACQUES 1	Good. The sun's setting. Good.

He heads off.

Someone walks to a microphone.

MIC	The sun set. Darkness fell. Presently, the chateau began to make itself strangely visible by some light of its own, as though it were growing luminous. Soon, from a score of the great windows, flames burst forth.

GABELLE is present.

SERVANT	Help, Gabelle, help! Help everyone.

The ROAD MENDER is stood there with the other villagers.

GABELLE	The chateau's on fire. Will you help us?
R MENDER	It must burn, Gabelle.

JACQUES ONE appears, the flames burning behind him. He nods towards GABELLE. Everyone moves in on GABELLE.

Someone walks towards a microphone.

MIC	**From Paris.**

We are in LORRY's bank in London.

CRUNCHER stands by LORRY's desk. CHARLES sits on the edge of it. There are a number of French Aristocrats there.

DARNAY	Tonight? And is anyone going with you?
LORRY	Jerry. No one will suspect Jerry of being anything but a British Bulldog – my bodyguard.

DARNAY   I wish I was going.

LORRY   You're French. That'd be total / madness.

DARNAY   It's because I'm French. I feel – like I've
              abandoned – something –

LORRY   The money and the documents that we are
              managing to get out of our Paris office, are
              brought by Frenchmen whose heads are
              hanging on by a hair.

He indicates to the aristocrats.

DARNAY   Then why go?

LORRY   France is safe enough for me. The consequences
              – if some of our documents were seized – well!
              I have to go.

He picks up a letter.

              I've shown this to everyone I can think of –
              including the French that have made their way
              here.

He reads.

              'To Monsieur, previously the Marquis
              Evremonde, of France.'

ARISTO 1   A degenerate.

ARISTO 2   Set himself against his uncle, the last
              Monseigneur Evremonde –

ARISTO 1   A total shit –

ARISTO 2   He's infected with the new doctrines –

ARISTO 1   Gave all his lands away to the herd –

ARISTO 2   A lover of scum –

ARISTO 1   Let's hope his beloved peasants tear him to
              pieces – that's all he deserves.

LORRY	No one seems to have a good word to say about this man or any idea where we could find him.
DARNAY	I know him.
LORRY	Really? Is he here in London?
DARNAY	I believe so.
LORRY	Could you get this to / him?
DARNAY	Yes. What time do you leave for Paris?
LORRY	Eight.
DARNAY	I'll come back to see you off.

DARNAY moves away. He tears into the letter. A television screen flickers on and GABELLE speaks from it.

GABELLE   Prison of the Abbaye, Paris. June 21st 1792.

Monsieur Charles.

I've been imprisoned. I'll be brought before a Tribunal. I'll lose my life; for the crime of 'Treason against the majesty of the people.' They won't listen when I tell them that I've acted *for* them according to your commands. They won't accept that you'd instructed me to collect no rent and to wipe all debts. They say I've acted for someone who abandoned France. I beg you to come and vouch for me. This prison is horror. And every hour here I'm nearer to my death. My fault, is that I've been true to you. I pray you'll be true to me.

Gabelle.

DARNAY returns to the bank and meets LORRY and CRUNCHER dressed ready for travel.

DARNAY	I delivered that letter. I didn't let him write a reply as it'd be too risky for you to carry. But will you take a verbal one?
LORRY	If it's not dangerous.
DARNAY	No. But it is to a prisoner in the Abbaye.
MR LORRY	What's his name?
DARNAY	Gabelle.
LORRY	And the message?
DARNAY	He's received the letter, and will come.

A grindstone turns. Metal is ground against it. Sparks fly into the air around it.

Someone walks towards a microphone.

MIC	**To Paris.**

DARNAY turns and faces a group of patriots in red caps and tri-coloured cockades.

He is in Paris.

A RED CAP comes from behind DARNAY and pushes him towards a table.

OFFICER	Papers, prisoner.

DARNAY hands the papers over.

DARNAY	I'm not a prisoner, I'm a free traveller and a French citizen.
OFFICER	You're the émigré, Evremonde?
DARNAY	Yes.
OFFICER	Welcome to Paris, Evremonde.

She laughs.

	You are consigned, Evremonde, to La Force prison.
DARNAY	Is this a joke? For what offence?
OFFICER	Since you were here, Evremonde, we have new laws and new offences.
DARNAY	I've come here voluntarily, in response to the written appeal you have there – an appeal from a fellow countryman – I've come to help him – is that not my right?
OFFICER	Tell him, Citizen Defarge.

DEFARGE steps forward out of the darkness.

Émigrés have no rights!

The OFFICER stamps a paper and hands it to DEFARGE.

DEFARGE	Émigrés have no rights, Evremonde.

He motions for DARNAY to follow him.

They move outside.

	Is it you who married Doctor Manette's daughter?
DARNAY	Yes.
DEFARGE	My name's Defarge, I keep a wine-shop in the suburb Saint Antoine.
DARNAY	My wife came to your house to see her father.
DEFARGE	Did you not hear that we have a sharp new lady in France – she's called The Guillotine – what the fuck brought you back here?
DARNAY	You just heard me say – to help a fellow citizen – don't you believe it?
DEFARGE	You're lost.

DARNAY	Will you help me?
DEFARGE	No.
DARNAY	This prison – will I be able to communicate with anyone outside?
DEFARGE	You'll find out.

Someone walks towards a microphone.

MIC **In Secret.**

A line of people appear in the dark.

A Gaoler appears.

GAOLER 1 What the fuck? How many more of them?

DEFARGE hands DARNAY's papers to the Gaoler.

In secret, too. As if I wasn't already full to bursting!

He files the paper.

Come with me, émigré.

DEFARGE disappears.

The line of people step forward, blinking into the dismal prison twilight.

Men and women, in ragged, aristocratic clothing are reading, writing, knitting, sewing, smoking – like ghosts of elegance.

They all make an individual verbal greeting or courtesy to DARNAY.

One steps forward.

ONE	In the name of the assembled companions in misfortune, I have the honour of welcoming you to La Force. Could I ask your name?
DARNAY	Charles Darnay.
GAOLER	The prisoner is the émigré Charles Evremonde.

ONE   But I hope…you are not in secret?

DARNAY   I don't know what that means, but I've heard
               them say it.

ONE   I'm sorry.

She turns to the line.

               In secret.

*The Gaoler takes DARNAY's arm and walks him along the line. They
all mutter commiserations to him as he passes.*

They disappear into the darkness.

DARNAY is taken into the shipping containers.

DARNAY   Where are we going?

GAOLER 1   They want you to 'ave your own cell.

DARNAY   Why?

GAOLER 1   The fuck do I know.

They continue to the top container.

Someone walks towards a microphone.

MIC   **The Grindstone.**

*A grindstone turns. Metal is ground against it. Sparks fly into the
air around it.*

A fire is lit.

JARVIS LORRY sits beside it. He works.

JERRY stands nearby.

LORRY   This city sounds and feels more dreadful every
               night.

CRUNCHER   God have mercy on all those who are in danger.

*Guards walk in, and through them rush LUCIE and MANETTE.
PROSS follows carrying LITTLE LUCIE.*

LORRY	What is this? What's brought you / here?
LUCIE	It's Charles.
LORRY	What about / Charles?
LUCIE	He's here.
LORRY	Here in Paris?
LUCIE	For three or four days – I'm not exactly – someone he knew – he wanted to help – he needed to come to France – he was stopped at the barrier and sent to prison.

A grindstone turns. Metal is ground against it. Sparks fly into the air around it.

MANETTE	What's that noise?
LORRY	Don't look. What prison is he in?
LUCIE	La Force.
LORRY	La Force!

A beat.

> Lucie; there's nothing you can do tonight. Please do as I ask. Would you – if I put you and Pross and Little Lucie in a room at the back here – leave your father and me alone –

LUCIE	No – why / should I?
LORRY	For two minutes?
LUCIE	No!
MANETTE	Please, Lucie. What have I promised you?

A beat. Then LUCIE nods.

LORRY gestures to JERRY who moves away with LUCIE, PROSS and LITTLE LUCIE.

LORRY takes MANETTE's arm and they stand and look towards another part of the stage.

The grindstone turns. Surrounding it are a group of men and women. Many of the men are stripped to the waist. All those gathered are covered in blood. They drink wine greedily. They look like devils lit only by the sparks of the grindstone. Even the hatchets, knives, bayonets, swords, that are passed to be sharpened, are red with blood. One woman – sat in the centre of this horror is breastfeeding her baby.

LORRY   They go back and forth to the prisons. And
            they murder the prisoners. This is what we
            face if we're to help Charles.

MANETTE   The risk is high, Lorry. Because Charles –
            he's an Evremonde – he's from an aristocratic
            family.

Silence.

LORRY   Of course. Of course – that's how he knew of
            Charles Evremonde when I asked about him.
            Then all our lives are in danger.

MANETTE   Let me talk to them.

LORRY   No.

MANETTE   I have a charmed life in this city. I was a
            prisoner in the Bastille – once they know / that

LORRY   It's a massive risk.

MANETTE   It's given me a power that brought us through
            the barrier, got us information about Charles
            – I can get him out of this. I've promised
            Lucie I'll do it.

He leaves the light around the table, and crosses, through the dark, to the group around the grindstone.

            There is no patriot in Paris, in France, who
            would touch me – except to embrace me or
            carry me in triumph – once he knew my name.

He stands amongst the group.

They shout his name.

ALL   Manette!

Suddenly they lift him into the air with roars of approval.

They sing 'La Carmagnole' as they carry him away.

Blackout.

Someone walks towards a microphone.

MIC   **Protection.**

The lights come up and LORRY, CRUNCHER, LUCIE, PROSS and LITTLE LUCIE are all stood in a group.

They stand a while – expectant.

DEFARGE appears before them.

LORRY takes a step towards him.

DEFARGE   Do you know me?

LUCIE   Yes of course – of course we know you.

LORRY   Have you been sent by Doctor Manette?

DEFARGE   Yes.

LORRY   And what does he say?

DEFARGE hands him a scrap of paper. LORRY reads.

                       He says he's in La Force with Charles. And
                       that they're safe.

LUCIE   Thank God.

PROSS   Yes, thank God.

LORRY   And that Defarge has a letter for you, Lucie,
                       from Charles.

DEFARGE hands a letter to LUCIE – he walks away for a moment.

LUCIE reads aloud.

LUCIE　　　　　'Lucie,
　　　　　　　　Take strength from this. I'm well, and your
　　　　　　　　father has influence here. You can't reply to
　　　　　　　　this letter. Kiss our girl for me.'

*DEFARGE returns with MADAME DEFARGE another woman,
CLÉMENCE.*

LORRY　　　　　This is Madame Defarge?

DEFARGE　　　　Yes. She's here so she can recognise you all.
　　　　　　　　It's for your safety.

MADAME DEFARGE begins to knit.

LUCIE goes over and touches DEFARGE's arm.

LUCIE　　　　　Thank you.

*She heads towards MADAME DEFARGE – but stops as MADAME
DEFARGE lifts her head and stares coldly at her. LUCIE steps back.*

MADAME D　　　Is that his child?

LORRY　　　　　Yes.

*LUCIE instinctively kneels on the ground and holds the child to her
breast.*

MADAME DEFARGE knits.

　　　　　　　　Lucie, Madame Defarge needs to see the
　　　　　　　　people she has the power to protect.

MADAME DEFARGE looks at DEFARGE.

MADAME D　　　It's enough. We can go.

LUCIE　　　　　Please help me to my husband. If you can.

MADAME D　　　Your husband's not my business here. It's the
　　　　　　　　daughter of your husband who's my business
　　　　　　　　here.

LUCIE   For my sake then. For my child's sake.

MADAME DEFARGE turns to go.

LUCIE   As a wife and mother – I beg you – with any
             power that you have – to use it – not – not
             against my husband – but to use it to help him.

MADAME D   You people are all the same. You don't
             recognise tragedy and pain 'til it's at your door.

MADAME DEFARGE turns to CLÉMENCE.

             Clémence, the wives and mothers we've
             known since we were as little as this child –
             smaller – we've known *their* husbands and
             fathers stuck in prison. All our lives, we've
             seen our sisters suffer – and their children –
             suffer poverty, nakedness, hunger, sickness,
             misery, oppression and neglect. Have we not?

CLÉMENCE   We've seen nothing else.

MADAME D looks back to LUCIE.

MADAME D   Sat in your home in Britain. Did you know,
             did you think, did you care?

No reply.

             So I ask you – is it likely that the trouble of one
             wife and mother would be much to us now?

She leaves, followed by CLÉMENCE and then DEFARGE.

PROSS runs after them.

*In the following MADAME DEFARGE and CLÉMENCE speak in
French, PROSS in English.*

PROSS   I don't understand a word of your awful
             language.

MADAME D   **What does this servant want?**

CLÉMENCE   **Liberation?**

The French women laugh.

PROSS   If I thought you were going to do any harm to
             my girls – I'll find you.

MADAME D   **Speak French or don't speak at all.**

CLÉMENCE   **Come with us – leave those arrogant fools.
             Come.**

DEFARGE   **Leave her.**

The all start to go. PROSS calls after them.

PROSS   You won't hurt them. I won't let you.

Someone walks towards a microphone.

MIC   **A Fever.**

*From wood and tools that are brought on during the following a
guillotine is built.*

MANETTE walks to another microphone.

MANETTE   There's a Tribunal that sits in La Force. What
             a group of men. They stank of murder. Each
             prisoner is brought in front of them and very
             quickly the order is given for the prisoner to
             be massacred or released. I told them who
             I was and about my eighteen years in the
             Bastille – and I was identified – by the man
             you found me with – who used to work for me
             – who took me in from the Bastille – Defarge
             – he was there – on the Tribunal – and he
             identified me. I told them about Charles –
             that he's my son-in-law, and they called for
             him. It felt like we were seconds away from
             his release – then – Defarge whispered to the
             others; then they said that Charles was to
             remain in custody, but, for my sake, he'd be
             kept safe.

What I saw – an d you must never tell
Lucie – the confusion – the speed of the
decisions – one man was freed – but those
who weren't…… I saw some savages – cutting
with swords – into a woman – cutting her into
pieces. What is this nightmare?

Everywhere I looked I saw tiny guillotines, on
chains around people's necks, lying on their
breast where once a cross would've been. The
Crucifix, the Guillotine – we bow down before
instruments of death.

There's a raging fever in the nation and in a
fever there is no pause, no pity, no peace.

The blade of the guillotine falls.

LUCIE falls to her knees and sobs.

The blade of the guillotine falls.

MANETTE goes to his daughter.

MANETTE   I know I can save him, Lucie.

He holds her and comforts her.

        And there's a way for him to see you.

LUCIE   How? How? Tell / me.

MANETTE   There's an upper window in the prison –
        sometimes – at about three in the afternoon –
        when he can get to it – he might see you in the
        street, if you stood in a certain place that I can
        show you.

She stands suddenly and is dressed for the outdoors by PROSS.

Music.

        But you won't be able to see him. And even if
        you could, it would be very dangerous to make
        any sign to him.

LUCIE has taken hold of LITTLE LUCIE's hand. They stand looking up.

My poor child.

We watch DARNAY in the top shipping-container.

LUCIE   Show me the place and I will go every day.

The weather changes around the two LUCIEs – PROSS brings changes of clothes for each season.

We end in winter. Snow falls. The LUCIEs have been dressed appropriately.

The ROAD MENDER is seen in another part of the stage.

He is sawing wood into lengths for burning.

A clock strikes four.

LUCIE turns to leave.

R MENDER   Good day, citizeness.

LUCIE   Good day, citizen.

R MENDER   Walking here again, citizeness?

LUCIE   You see me, citizen.

The ROAD MENDER glances at the prison, points at the prison, and puts his ten fingers before his face to represent bars and then peeps through them.

R MENDER   But it's not my business. My business is the
               sawing of wood for fires. Though it used to be
               the mending of roads. By a village you might
               know, citizeness.

LUCIE   Why would you think that?

R MENDER   Aww! A child too! Your mother, is it not, my
               little citizeness?

LITTLE L   Do I say yes, mamma?

LUCIE	Yes, darling.
LITTLE L	Yes, citizen.
R MENDER	Aww! See my saw! I call it my Little Guillotine.

He saws and sings.

Tum Tum Tum! And off his head will come!

A piece of wood falls into his basket. He picks up another piece. Marks the length for cutting.

And now his wife.

He saws and sings.

Doo, Doo, Doo! And off *her* head comes too!

A piece of wood falls into his basket. He picks up another piece. Marks the length for cutting.

Now, a child.

He saws and sings.

Hee Hee Hee! All the fa-mi-lee!

A piece of wood falls into his basket.

But it's not my business!

He moves away with his basket.

LUCIE moves to go, but her father rushes to them.

MANETTE	Lucie, I was just with Charles – he's summoned for to-morrow.
LUCIE	For to-morrow?
MANETTE	He'll be in front of the Tribunal. Then he'll be with you again. I've made sure of it.
LUCIE	Thank you, Father. Thank you.
MANETTE	I must see Lorry.

He turns in another direction. CRUNCHER appears before him.

> Tell Lorry that Charles will be summoned in
> front of the Tribunal tomorrow.

JERRY takes a few steps through the space to where LORRY is working.

CRUNCHER   Summoned tomorrow.

LORRY calls out.

LORRY   Did you hear that?

CARLTON appears from the dark. Drinking from a large, full glass.

CARTON   Yes. Tomorrow.

Someone walks towards a microphone.

MIC   **Triumph.**

The Tribunal has formed, on it sits a PRESIDENT and two JUDGES.

*Watching from the front row of an audience are DEFARGE, MADAME
DEFARGE, MANETTE and LORRY.*

DARNAY steps forward onto a designated spot.

PRESIDENT 1 Charles Evremonde, called Darnay?

DARNAY   Yes.

JUDGE 1   You are accused as an émigré, whose life is
             forfeit to the Republic, under the decree which
             banished all émigrés on pain of Death.

JUDGE 2   Is it true that you have lived in Britain for
             many years?

DARNAY   It is.

JUDGE 2   So you're an émigré?

DARNAY   Not within the sense and spirit of the new laws.

JUDGE 2   Why not?

DARNAY   I left this country before the word émigré had
              the meaning that your Tribunal attaches to it.
              I voluntarily gave up a title that I didn't believe
              in – that I despised. I lived in Britain and
              worked rather than live on profit my family
              made from abusing the people of France.

PRESIDENT   And what proof do you have of this?

DARNAY   I have two witnesses; Theophile Gabelle, and
              Alexandre Manette.

The audience cheer MANETTE's name.

JUDGE 2   And you married in Britain, did you not?

DARNAY   Yes, but to a French woman; Lucie Manette,
              the only daughter of Doctor Manette, who sits
              there.

PRESIDENT   Why did you return to France when you did,
              and not sooner?

DARNAY   Because I had no way of living in France, I'd
              given all that away. In Britain, I can live by
              teaching French. I came back at the request
              of a French citizen, with the hope of saving his
              life.

PRESIDENT   And what is the name of this citizen?

DARNAY   Theopile Gabelle. The citizen's letter was
              taken from me at the barrier but I believe it is
              amongst the papers that Citizen Doctor
              Manette prepared on my behalf.

JUDGE ONE passes the letter to the PRESIDENT.

The PRESIDENT reads.

A screen flickers to life. GABELLE appears as before.

GABELLE   They won't listen when I repeatedly tell them
              that I've acted *for* them according to your

commands. They won't accept that you'd instructed me to collect no rent and to wipe all debts.

GABELLE has taken his place to give evidence to the court.

JUDGE 2   You are Citizen Gabelle?

GABELLE   Yes Citizen.

PRESIDENT   You are free?

GABELLE   Yes, I was freed from the Prison of the Abbaye, when the Tribunal declared themselves satisfied that the accusation against me was answered, by the surrender of the citizen Evremonde, called Darnay.

JUDGE 2   And can you confirm the claims made here?

The JUDGE holds up the letter.

GABELLE   Yes... Citizen Evremonde is an honourable man and friend of The Republic's cause.

Time jump.

He stands aside and MANETTE takes his place.

MANETTE   You all know me as the Doctor who survived eighteen years as a prisoner of the Bastille. I imagine that those that imprisoned me were the kind of men, the enemies of France, that the Republic has sought to drive from our country. Charles Darnay is not such a man. When I was released from the Bastille and handed to our friends, Citizen and Citizeness Defarge, I went into exile for my safety – to survive. The same can be said of Charles Darnay. He was my first friend in exile – and don't assume he was escaping to the sympathies of the British aristocratic government. In fact he's been tried for his life

as an enemy of it. He is an honest man –
a good man – he thought nothing of his own
life when he came to France to fight for the
release of Citizen Gabelle and was a friend to
all of those who once worked on the estates of
his hated family. Hated by him also. A name
he has cast off. He has abandoned that idea
of France. Would I have given him my only
daughter if he was sympathetic to those tyrants
– to the monsters that tortured me for eighteen
years. Citizens – you have held me in your
hearts – I hold this man in mine. I ask you –
as you forge the new France – to see the value
in this man's life – to see what he has done
for France and what he might do. Allow him
to be Charles Darnay a Citizen of our great
Republic.

The audience are stirred and cheer.

The JUDGE silences them by lifting his hand.

PRESIDENT   We have heard enough and are ready to vote.

JUDGE 1   Not guilty.

AUDIENCE   Long live the Republic.

JUDGE 2   Not guilty.

AUDIENCE   Long live the Republic.

PRESIDENT   Not guilty.

AUDIENCE   Long live the Republic.

PRESIDENT   The accused is free to go. Long live the Republic.

Beautiful music plays.

During the following, a simple home is built around the family:

DARNAY is stunned. MANETTE moves to him and holds him in his arms.

MANETTE turns DARNAY to face LUCIE.

LUCIE and DARNAY run to each other and hold each other.

PROSS brings LITTLE LUCIE forward and DARNAY bends down and takes her in his arms.

Once it's built; the family move happily and freely around the home.

The condemned men are pushed over to the car.

MIC   **A Knock at the Door.**

In the MANETTE home, CHARLES and LUCIE are reading. MANETTE is sleeping in a chair. LITTLE LUCIE sleeps on his lap.

PROSS and JERRY are preparing to go out.

CRUNCHER   It would be so much easier – if either of us had a bit of French. I would've thought...

He nods towards PROSS.

PROSS   What?

CRUNCHER   You livin' with a French family all o' these years –

PROSS   I'm pleased to say I know no more of that nonsense than you do. I can deal with their shopkeepers, that's all that matters. If the shopkeeper holds up three fingers for a piece of cheese you hold up two – that's a fair price. *(To LUCIE.) Now*, Ladybird, don't you move from that fire 'til I come back! Take care of that husband you have back with you.

LUCIE puts her head on DARNAY's shoulder.

              Doctor Manette, are you awake?

MANETTE   No.

PROSS   Very funny. Can I ask you a question?

MANETTE   Can I stop you?

PROSS   Is there any chance yet, of our getting out of
              this place?

MANETTE   Not yet. Not until we have papers for Charles.

PROSS   Oh, well. Then we must have patience. We
              must hold up our heads and fight low, as my
              brother Solomon used to say. Ready, Jerry!

JERRY   Ready!

JERRY and PROSS leave.

LITTLE LUCIE wakes up.

MANETTE   Hello darling, girl.

LITTLE LUCIE starts.

LITTLE L   Where's Daddy?

LUCIE   He's here.

DARNAY   I'm just here.

LITTLE L   I was scared.

MANETTE   Of what?

LITTLE L   I don't know – I just feel……

MANETTE   I brought your Daddy home. He's safe – we're
              all safe now.

LUCIE   Don't be scared. Come here and I'll read to
              you.

MANETTE   No – I know what – I have a story for you.

LUCIE   Good. Go on then.

MANETTE   Once upon a time, there was a –

Suddenly LUCIE jumps to her feet.

LUCIE   What's that?

MANETTE   Lucie, it's nothing. Just – try and be calm.

LUCIE	I thought that I heard feet on the stairs.

The guillotine falls.

	The door. Oh, God.
DARNAY	Lucie – calm down.
LITTLE L	I don't like it.
LUCIE	Look out of the door.
MANETTE	I'll go.
LUCIE	Charles – hide. Save him / please.
MANETTE	Lucie – enough! I have saved him.

He moves across the space and JACQUES ONE, CLÉMENCE and a RED CAP appear from the dark.

They hold weapons.

RED CAP	The Citizen Evremonde, called Darnay.
DARNAY	Who wants him?
RED CAP	I know you, Evremonde – I saw you before the Tribunal yesterday.
	You're to be taken again as a prisoner of the Republic.

The three move in on DARNAY. LUCIE and LITTLE LUCIE cling to him.

DARNAY	Tell me how and why.
JACQUES 1	You just need to know you're returning to La Force.
LUCIE	No please no.
MANETTE	Do you know me?
RED CAP	Yes.
LUCIE	Father, do / something.

CLÉMENCE   We all know you, Citizen Doctor.

MANETTE   Then answer me please. Why is this
             happening?

RED CAP   He's been denounced by the Section of Saint
             Antoine.

MANETTE   And accused of what?

A JACQUES   Don't ask any more. Evremonde, move!

MANETTE   Will you tell me who's denounced him?

CLÉMENCE   The Citizen and Citizeness Defarge. And one
             other.

DARNAY   What other?

A JACQUES   You'll be answered to-morrow.

DARNAY is taken away.

Someone walks towards a microphone.

MIC   **A Hand at Cards.**

A wine-shop is created.

People sat drinking. Some in red caps.

PROSS and JERRY approach. JERRY is carrying everything.

CRUNCHER   We've got everything except the wine.

PROSS   I know – but these wine-shops!

CRUNCHER   This looks quieter than most of 'em.

PROSS   It's red with red caps.

She shakes her head.

             But not as red as some. Come on.

She heads in.

The wine-shop comes vibrantly to life as she steps into it.

As she makes her way towards the shopkeeper, BARSAD gets up from his feet and turns towards her.

She stops and screams.

All stand, thinking violence has occurred.

BARSAD   *(Quietly.)* What the fuck are you doin'?

PROSS   Solomon. Solo / mon.

BARSAD   Don't call me that. My name is John

*He looks at the Red Caps. And then in **French**:*

My name is John.

PROSS   I don't believe it. Where have you been?

BARSAD   Come outside!

They move out.

PROSS   How come you're here? In Paris?

BARSAD   Shuttup! D'ya wanna get me killed?

PROSS bursts into tears.

PROSS   How could you ask me such a question?

She touches his face.

My brother.

BARSAD nods toward JERRY.

BARSAD   Who's this? What you fuckin' lookin' at me
           like that for?

JERRY shrugs.

BARSAD looks back to his sister.

Now leave me.

He turns to go. She pulls him back.

PROSS   What? Why would you talk to me like this?
          Like you hate me. All I've ever done is try to
          love you. Please – just show me – any – just a
          tiny bit of affection.

A beat.

He gives her the quickest of kisses.

BARSAD   There. Will that do yer?

PROSS puts down her head and weeps.

          If you expect me to be surprised – I'm not. I
          knew you were here. I know of most people
          who are here. If you really don't want to put
          me in danger – then go – now. I'm an official.

PROSS   Solomon – you had the makings in you to be
          the best of men. An official? Among – such
          people?

BARSAD   I knew it. You want me killed. I'll be labelled
          Suspected – because of my own fucking sister.
          I'm trying to get on here – I'm doing well.

JERRY taps him on the shoulder.

CRUNCHER Can I ask if your name is Solomon John or
          John Solomon?

BARSAD   What?

CRUNCHER She's your sister and she calls you Solomon –
          and I know you as John. And her surname is
          Pross. That wasn't your name back / over the
          water.

BARSAD   What you talkin' about?

CRUNCHER I'd swear it's you. You're the spy.

PROSS   What?

BARSAD   You wanna shut your face.

CRUNCHER   You were a witness at Charles Darnay's trial at
            the Bailey. What was your name?

CARTON has appeared from the darkness.

CARTON   Barsad!

CRUNCHER   That's it. That's the name.

CARTON   Don't be scared, Pross. I arrived at Lorry's
            last night. We agreed to keep it to ourselves
            until I could be useful. I wish you had a better
            employed brother than Mr Barsad. I wish for
            your sake he wasn't a spy for the prisons.

BARSAD   Who do you think / you're fuckin'

CARTON   I saw you coming out of the prison an hour or
            so ago. You have a face to be remembered,
            and I was curious – so I followed you
            into the wine-shop here, and I listened to
            your conversations. And thank you – because
            listening to you – thoughts I have – began to
            shape into a plan.

BARSAD   What plan?

CARTON   Let's go where we can talk.

BARSAD   Or? What?

CARTON   Really, Mr Barsad, I can't say if you can't.

BARSAD   Is that some sort of threat?

SOLOMON turns on his sister.

            If any trouble comes to me from this –

CARTON   Barsad, it's only because of the respect I have
            for your sister that I'll make a proposal for our
            mutual benefit. Will you come?

BARSAD   I'll hear what you've got to say. Yes.

They cross to where LORRY sits by a fire.

The wine-shop, PROSS and CRUNCHER disappear.

CARTON   Pross' brother. Mr Barsad.

LORRY   Barsad? I feel like I know the name – and the face.

CARTON   I told you you had a remarkable face, Barsad. Witness at the Old Bailey trial. Sit down.

Barsad and Carton sit.

       Barsad has been recognised by Pross as the brother you will have heard of. And – Darnay has been taken back to prison.

LORRY   What? I left him safe and free – just – two hours ago.

CARTON   When was it done, Barsad?

BARSAD   Last hour or so.

CARTON   And I know, from Barsad's communication to a fellow spy over a bottle of wine, that the arrest has taken place. He left the officers at the gate, and saw them enter the building.

LORRY sits and puts his hands to his head.

       You said he would go before a Tribunal again tomorrow?

BARSAD   Yes.

CARTON   It worries me, Lorry, the Doctor not having the power to prevent his arrest.

LORRY   Yes.

CARTON   So…this is a desperate time, when desperate games are played for desperate stakes. Now, the stake I have decided to play for is a friend in La Force. I want to win you, Mr Barsad.

BARSAD	You'll need good cards.
CARTON	I'll look over them. I'll see what I hold. Lorry, any chance of a little brandy?

LORRY puts a bottle and glass by him.

CARTON pours and drinks a glassful.

He holds up his hands as though looking at a hand of cards.

Mr Barsad: Spy for the prisons, employed
by the republican French government,
also employed by the aristocratic British
government, the enemy of France and
freedom. A double agent. That's an excellent
card. Mr. Barsad?

No response.

Look over your hand and see what you have.

CARTON pours and drinks a glassful of brandy.

Will you play?

BARSAD	I would have thought – that – your respect for my sister.
CARTON	The best way to show respect for your sister would be to finally relieve her of you! A foreigner, with aristocratic sympathies! A strong card – a guillotine card! Do you play?
BARSAD	No. Listen – this proposal of yours – I go on duty soon so can't stay much longer – what do you want?
CARTON	You hold keys for La Force?
BARSAD	An escape isn't possible.
CARTON	Haven't mentioned escape. You hold keys?
BARSAD	No. But – I can pass in and out when I choose.

CARTON stands.

CARTON Come into the other room – let's have one final word alone.

CARTON and BARSAD move up into the dark.

Someone walks towards a microphone.

MIC **The Game Made.**

CARTON and BARSAD move back into the light.

CARTON You stick to our arrangement and you've nothing to fear from me.

BARSAD leaves.

LORRY What is the arrangement?

CARTON If Darnay's found guilty, I've made sure that I'll have access to him.

LORRY Access to him? That won't save him.

CARTON I never said it would.

Pause.

LORRY puts his face in his hands and sobs.

CARTON gently puts his hand on his shoulder.

  Don't tell Lucie about any of this. She'll think a thousand things, and it'll only add to her fears. She must be devastated. You should go to her.

LORRY I'm going now.

CARTON Good. She's very attached to you. How does she look?

LORRY Anxious and unhappy, but always very beautiful.

CARTON That beauty.

CARTON turns his back to LORRY,

>I forgot it.

He turns back.

>And your work here – all done?

LORRY   I've done all I can. I'd hoped to have seen
          them safe, and then to have left Paris. I have
          my Leave To Pass.

CARTON   Yours is a long life to look back on.

LORRY   I'm seventy-eight.

CARTON   See what a place you fill at seventy-eight. How
          many people will miss you when you leave it
          empty?

LORRY   A solitary old bachelor. No one will weep for
          me.

CARTON   How can you say that? Wouldn't she weep for
          you? Wouldn't her child?

LORRY   Yes, yes, thank God.

CARTON   God has nothing to do with it. Where is God
          now? It's about you and what you have done.
          If you felt – that in your seventy-eight years –
          you'd – done nothing – of use – of good – to be
          remembered by; if you hadn't put yourself into
          the heart of another human being – you'd feel
          lonely tonight wouldn't you and your seventy-
          eight years would feel like seventy-eight curses.

LORRY   Yes. They would.

Silence.

CARTON   You must go to her. Let's go.

They move towards the dark.

I promise I'll be at the Court tomorrow.
I'll be there but hidden amongst the crowd.
But tonight – you told me there was a spot
where she waited…

CARTON moves to the exact same spot as LUCIE earlier.

LORRY   Yes – we'll pass it. I can show you.

CARTON   Thank you.

A light comes up on DARNAY; in the top shipping container, as before.

Music.

LORRY   She came here every day.

LORRY moves into the dark.

CARTON   That she would stand here every day –
knowing she would never see him, but that he
might see her.

For some time we watch both men in these different spaces.

The ROAD MENDER is seen in another part of the stage.

The music disappears and CARTON moves past the ROAD MENDER.

CARTON   Good night, citizen.

R MENDER   Good night, citizen.

CARTON   How goes the Republic?

R MENDER   You mean the guillotine? Not bad. The Lady
shaved sixty-three to-day. Tum Tum Tum –
And off your head will come.

He laughs.

CARTON   Do you go a lot?

R MENDER   Always. Every day. That Lady. What a
barber. Sixty-three!

Have you been?

CARTON   Never.

CARTON turns away.

Good night, citizen.

He moves away.

R MENDER   Good night, citizen.

The ROAD MENDER calls after him.

Go and see The Lady!

A chemists is built.

CARTON hands the CHEMIST a scrap of paper.

The CHEMIST whistles.

CHEMIST   Iy, iy, iy!

She looks at CARTON, who avoids her gaze.

For you, citizen?

CARTON   Yes.

CHEMIST   You need to be very careful to keep them
              separate. You know what can happen if you
              mix them?

CARTON   Yes.

The CHEMIST disappears into the dark.

There is nothing more to do.

The CHEMIST re-appears and hands over two small packets.

Then she disappears into the dark.

A cold light is on CARTON.

MIC   He stood upon a bridge listening to the
              water as it splashed the river-walls of Paris.
              He looked to the moon, shining bright; but

> looking, now, to him, like a dead face in the
> sky. He stood for hours like this.

The music is achingly beautiful.

The lights are as a magnificent sunrise.

> But, as the glorious sun rose, it seemed to strike
> out the burden of the night, and somehow
> warm his heart. A bridge of light appeared to
> span the air between him and the sun. And he
> resolved – this is right – this is what I must do.

Someone walks to another microphone.

MIC **The Paper.**

A Tribunal has formed.

CARTON is hidden amongst those gathered to watch…

MANETTE and LUCIE sit together.

LORRY is also there.

DARNAY steps forward onto a designated spot.

LUCIE stands and they stare at each other.

MANETTE gently pulls LUCIE back to sitting.

PRESIDENT 2 Charles Evremonde, called Darnay?

DARNAY Yes.

JUDGE 3 reads from notes.

JUDGE 3 Charles Evremonde, called Darnay. Released
yesterday. Re-accused and retaken yesterday.
Suspected and Denounced as an enemy of the
Republic, as an Aristocrat, as one of a family
of tyrants, who used their privileges to the
oppression of the people. It is demanded that
Charles Evremonde, called Darnay, in the light
of such charges should be sentenced to Death
in Law.

There is muttering in the audience.

JUDGE 4   Was the Accused openly denounced or secretly?

JUDGE 3   Openly.

PRESIDENT 2 By whom?

JUDGE 3   Three people. Ernest Defarge, wine-vendor of St. Antoine.

PRESIDENT 2 Good.

JUDGE 3   Thérèse Defarge, his wife.

PRESIDENT 2 Good.

JUDGE 3   Alexandre Manette, physician.

There is suddenly uproar in the court.

MANETTE slowly stands. He is shaking his head.

MANETTE   President, this is a lie – you know the accused is my daughter's husband. She means more to me than life. Where / is the liar?

PRESIDENT 2 Citizen Manette, be calm. As to what means more to you than life – if the Republic should demand you sacrifice your child herself, your duty would be to sacrifice her. Listen to what is to follow. Call Ernest Defarge.

OFFICER   Ernest Defarge!

DEFARGE takes his place as witness.

JUDGE 4   You knew Alexandre Manette at the time of his imprisonment?

DEFARGE   We didn't know he was imprisoned – he disappeared – but I worked for him at that time, yes.

JUDGE 4   And at the time of his release you took responsibility for him.

DEFARGE   Yes.

JUDGE 4   What state was he in at that time?

DEFARGE   He was sick. Mind sick. He'd wasted away.
               He had no memories of who he was before the
               Bastille.

PRESIDENT 2   You did good service at the taking of the Bastille,
               citizen?

DEFARGE   I believe so.

MADAME DEFARGE calls out.

MADAME D   You were one of the best patriots there! You
               were one of the first to enter when it fell.

Cheers from the audience.

JUDGE 3   Inform the Tribunal of what you did that day
               within the Bastille, citizen.

DEFARGE   I knew the Citizen Doctor had been confined
               in a cell known as One Hundred and Five,
               North Tower. I promised myself that when
               the place fell I'd examine that cell. We were
               – directed by a jailer. We examine the cell
               very closely. In a hole in the chimney, I find a
               written paper.

He takes it from his pocket.

               I've looked at some examples of the Doctor's
               handwriting. It matches.

The OFFICER takes the paper and takes it over to the PRESIDENT.

The PRESIDENT doesn't take it.

PRESIDENT 2   Let it be read.

*There is dead silence as the OFFICER returns it to DEFARGE. He
unfolds it.*

DEFARGE   I, Alexandre Manette, write this paper in my cell
           in the Bastille, during the last month of the year,
           1767. I hope one day, that some one may find it
           and read it with pity. I solemnly declare that my
           memory is exact, and that I write the truth.

           One night, in December in the year 1757, I
           was walking by the Seine when a carriage
           came along behind me, driven very fast. As I
           stood aside to let it pass a head was put out of
           the window, and a voice called to the driver
           to stop. Two climbed out of the door. They
           were both wrapped in cloaks, and appeared to
           hide themselves. The first said 'You are Doctor
           Manette?', 'We've been to your home,' said the
           second, 'and we were told that you were walking
           in this direction.' As they stood side by side, I
           saw that they both seemed very much like each
           other, in manner, voice, and (as far as I could
           see) face too. The first said 'Please – get into the
           carriage.' 'Gentlemen, I usually ask who seeks
           my assistance and the nature of the case. The
           reply to this came from the second. 'Doctor,
           your clients are people of importance. Our
           confidence in your skill assures us that you'll
           ascertain the nature of the case. Now – please
           get in.' I felt I had no choice. They climbed
           in after me. The carriage turned around, and
           drove on. We passed the North Barrier, and
           emerged on the country road. After some
           time, just as we'd passed through a village with
           a fountain, we stopped at a dark, magnificent
           chateau. We got out and walked towards it and
           I could hear what sounded like distressed cries
           of a woman. They rang the bell at the door.
           It was opened. The woman's cries grew louder
           as we climbed the stairs. I was shown into a
           room and I found a patient in a high fever of the
           brain, lying on a bed.

Music.

The bed has appeared in court. A young woman in it. Her arms are bound to her sides. MANETTE makes his way over to it. The two brothers approach; the 'first' is MONSEIGNEUR, the 'second' is his twin, the Marquis. Their faces are still partly covered.

> She was a young woman, not much past twenty; and incredibly beautiful. Her arms were bound to her sides with sashes and scarves. On one scarf, I saw the coat of arms of a Noble, and the letter E.

Only candles now light the intimate scene around the bed.

The woman's eyes are wild and dilated. She writhes around. Her breathing is panicked and uneven.

She constantly utters piercing shrieks. Then:

Y WOMAN   My husband, my father, and my brother! 1 – 2
– 3 – 4 – 5 – 6 – 7 –8 – 9 – 10 – 11 – 12. Hush!

She pauses and listens.

Then the shrieks and the writhing begin again.

MANETTE places his hands gently on her chest, in an attempt to calm her.

MANETTE   How long has she been like this?

MONSEIGN   Since about this time last night.

Y WOMAN   My husband, my father, and my brother! 1 – 2
– 3 – 4 – 5 – 6 – 7 –8 – 9 – 10 – 11 – 12. Hush!

She pauses and listens.

Then the shrieks and the writhing begin again.

MANETTE   She has a husband, a father, and a brother?

MONSEIGN   A brother.

MANETTE   And is that you?

MONSEIGN   No.

MANETTE   And the number twelve?

MARQUIS   Twelve o'clock.

MANETTE   If I'd known what I'd see, I could have come
with the medicines needed.

MONSEIGN   There's a case of medicines here.

Y WOMAN   My husband, my father, and my brother!

The Marquis hands the case to MANETTE.

Y WOMAN   1 – 2 – 3 – 4 – 5 –

MANETTE opens it and inspects the contents.

Y WOMAN   – 6 – 7 – 8 – 9 – 10 – 11 – 12. Hush!

She pauses and listens.

MANETTE   I can use these.

The young woman shrieks and the writhing begins again.

MANETTE pours contents from a bottle on to a spoon.

He struggles but forces her to swallow.

He does the same with contents from a second.

He then puts his hands back on her chest.

Y WOMAN   My husband, my father, and my brother! 1 – 2
– 3

She begins to slow down.

          – 4 – 5 – 6 – 7……

She settles and closes her eyes.

Silence.

MONSEIGN   There's another patient.

MANETTE   Urgent?

MONSEIGN   You'd better see.

MONSEIGNEUR picks up a light and moves away. MANETTE follows.

On the ground – a cushion under his head – lies a BOY of about seventeen.

The BOY's stomach is bleeding – his clothes drenched with the blood.

As MANETTE approaches the BOY pulls away in agony.

MONSEIGN   A crazed young common dog! A serf! He forced
                 my brother to draw upon him.

MANETTE   My poor boy. I'm a doctor. Let me examine it.

The BOY nods.

BOY   Doctor, they take what they want, humiliate us,
                 beat us, kill us; but we have a little pride left,
                 sometimes. She – have you seen her, Doctor?

MANETTE   I've seen her.

BOY   She's my sister, Doctor. They've had their
                 rights, these Nobles, with our sisters, for many
                 years. She was a good girl. She was married to
                 a good lad, too. We're all tenants of that man
                 who stands there. The other's his brother – the
                 worst of a bad race.

MANETTE is applying some lotion to the wound and dressing it.

The BOY struggles to speak.

                 We've been so robbed by that man who stands
                 there, taxed by him without mercy, made to
                 work without pay, they'd take anything from
                 us. Our father told us we should pray for our
                 women to be barren.

He winces with pain.

She'd not been married many weeks, when
that man's brother saw her and wanted her.
But my sister's good and she hated him.
So they used her husband to persuade her.
They harnessed him to a cart and drove him
like a dog. They kept him out in their grounds
all night, keeping the fucking frogs quiet so
their noble sleep wasn't disturbed. They kept
him out in the night, and in his harness all day.
For days. For nights. But he never asked her
to give in. Then one day at noon he was taken
out of harness – she was on the ground with
him – holding him close – as the bell struck
twelve – he let out these awful sounds – like
deep sobs – with every stroke of the bell.
Then he died in her arms.

Then this man's brother took her away.
To do whatever he wanted to do. My father's
heart burst. He's broken and silent. I took my
younger sister to a place where they'll never
find her and use her. Then last night I climbed
in. I went for him with the sword to make him
draw. My sister had run in...and...well... I'm
sorry she saw him cut me down. She started
screaming – and hasn't stopped.

Doctor, lift me up.

*MANETTE starts to lift him but the BOY finds the power to raise
himself.*

He touches his wound.

Arrghhh!

*He makes a cross in the air, in the direction of the First, with his
bloodied fingers.*

Monseigneur, I mark this cross of blood upon
you. All these things will be answered for; by

> you and your brother and all yours, to the last
> of your bad race.

As the hand drops so does he.

MANETTE lays him down dead. He slowly stands and looks at MONSEIGNEUR.

MONSEIGNEUR takes up the light and they move back to the young woman's bed.

The Marquis is staring down at her.

She lies still.

MANETTE checks her pulse and breath.

MONSEIGN   Is she dead?

MANETTE   Not yet. But she will die.

MONSEIGN   Doctor, the things you see here, are not to be
             spoken of.

MANETTE checks the young woman.

> Do you hear me?

MANETTE   Anything a patient says is heard in confidence.

He is still engaged in checking his patient.

> She's gone.

MONSEIGNEUR turns to the Marquis.

MONSEIGN   I'm sorry, brother.

He turns back to MANETTE. He holds out a large purse.

MANETTE   Excuse me – but – under the circumstances, no.

We are back with DEFARGE.

DEFARGE   In the morning I decided to write to the
             Minister, stating the nature of the two cases
             and stating all the circumstances.

The brothers and the bodies disappear and MANETTE re-takes his place at the Tribunal.

I'd just finished the letter, when I was told a young lady had called and asked to see me.

She was incredibly distressed. She was the wife of the second brother. She told me their name was Evremonde. She'd discovered the main facts of the story and her husband's share in it. She knew there was a younger sister and wanted to find and help her. She was a good, compassionate woman and was scared of her husband and his brother.

When I saw her back to her carriage, there was a little boy of two to three years old. 'For his sake, Doctor,' she said, pointing to him in tears, 'I'll do all I can to make amends. And I'll make him swear that he'll try to find the sister.' She kissed the boy, and said, 'It's for your own sake, Charles.'

Their carriage left and I never saw her again.

I went back in and added the name Evremonde to the letter. I delivered it myself that day.

That night, I was with my beautiful pregnant wife – her head was on my shoulder as we sat by the fire, when a man rang at my gate, and asked me to attend an urgent case in the Rue St. Honore. When I was clear of the house, a scarf was pulled tightly over my mouth from behind, and my arms held. The two brothers crossed the road from a dark corner, and identified me with a single gesture. The second one took my letter from his pocket, and burnt it in front of my face. I was brought here to the Bastille.

> I believe that that red cross marked in blood
> is fatal to those brothers, and that they have
> no part in God's mercies. So I, Alexandre
> Manette, denounce them and the last of their
> race, to the time when all shall be answered for
> in Heaven and on earth.

DEFARGE looks up from the paper.

The audience begin a terrible chant.

AUDIENCE BLOOD – BLOOD – BLOOD etc.

The chant continues under the following.

PRESIDENT 2 Let us hear the verdict of the judges.

JUDGE 3 Guilty.

A roar from the audience.

JUDGE 4 Guilty.

A roar from the audience.

PRESIDENT 2 Guilty.

A roar and then a return to the chant.

AUDIENCE BLOOD – BLOOD – BLOOD etc.

PRESIDENT 2 At heart and by descent an Aristocrat and enemy of the Republic; back to La Force, and death within twenty-four hours!

Someone walks towards a microphone.

MIC **Dusk.**

The court dissolves.

Music.

LUCIE runs towards her husband.

LUCIE Please let me hold him – just once! Please.

He is held by the RED CAPS and BARSAD.

BARSAD   Let her hold him. *(To DARNAY.)* You have
              seconds.

DARNAY   Goodbye, beautiful darling of my soul.

LUCIE   I will bear it, Charles. Don't suffer for me.

MANETTE falls to his knees and puts his face in his hands.

MANETTE   What have I done?

DARNAY   Nothing.

He lifts MANETTE to his feet.

              You should never kneel to us.

He grabs LUCIE.

DARNAY   We shall meet again at rest.

He is pulled away.

LUCIE   What shall I say to Lucie?

DARNAY   I don't know – I'm sorry – I / don't know

LUCIE   This will kill me.

DARNAY   Say goodbye to her for me.

LUCIE   It'll kill me – she'll be on her own.

DARNAY has gone.

She collapses. She fits.

LORRY tries to hold her.

CARTON sweeps her up.

CARTON   I'll take her to her coach.

He moves away with her.

LORRY helps MANETTE to his feet.

MANETTE   He will die.

LORRY   Yes. He will die.

The guillotine falls.

Someone walks towards a microphone.

MIC   **Darkness.**

The DEFARGE's wine-shop emerges.

There are no customers, only the DEFARGEs, A JACQUES and CLÉMENCE.

JACQUES 1   It's true what your wife says, 'why stop?'

DEFARGE   You have to stop somewhere.

MADAME D   At extermination.

JACQUES 1   Exactly.

DEFARGE   But this Doctor has suffered so much; you've
              seen him to-day; you saw his face when the
              paper was read.

MADAME D   I saw his face as not the face of a true friend /
              of the Republic.

DEFARGE   And you've seen the pain of his daughter,
              which must / be pain to him!

MADAME D   If it was up to you – you would free this
              Evremonde even now.

DEFARGE   No. I wouldn't. But I would say, stop there.

MADAME D   Listen, Jacques – Clèmence……listen. When
              the Bastille fell, and he found the paper that
              was read at the court today, he brings it home,
              and in the middle of the night, we read it, here
              on this spot. That night, I tell him, when we'd
              read the whole thing, that I have – my own
              secret. I told him,

She shakes with emotion.

> 'Defarge, I was brought up among fishermen,
> because that peasant family that was destroyed
> by the Evremonde brothers, is my family.
> Defarge, that sister and brother were my sister
> and brother, that was my sister's husband, that
> was my father, those dead are my dead. And
> that curse, made with that cross of blood, my
> blood, for that race to answer for those things,
> passes to me!' Ask him, is that true?

DEFARGE   It's true.

MADAME DEFARGE is sobbing, choking almost.

MADAME D   All of that race. All. Then tell Wind and Fire
            where to stop, but don't tell me.

A light comes up on DARNAY writing in his cell.

Elsewhere LORRY paces in his room.

Someone walks towards a microphone.

MIC   **Darker Still**.

The wine-shop disappears as CARTON approaches LORRY.

CARTON   How is she?

LORRY   Lost. I'll go back to her as soon as we're
            finished here. Manette thinks there might be
            one last / chance.

CARTON   Listen.

They both listen.

From somewhere in the darkness they hear:

MANETTE   I can't find it and I need it. Where is it?

LORRY   No. Please, God, no.

MANETTE appears.

MANETTE   Where's my bench? I can't find it. What have
           they done with my work? Time's running out
           – I must finish those shoes.

He is weeping now.

           Let me get to work.

He pulls his hair and stamps his feet.

           Please don't torture me.

LORRY   Sit down, old friend please.

LORRY strokes MANETTE's arm.

CARTON brings a chair over.

CARTON   We promise you – you'll soon have your bench
           and can work.

LORRY   Just sit for now.

MANETTE stares at CARTON. Then sits.

CARTON   So – no last chance.

LORRY   No. He'd better be taken to Lucie.

CARTON   Yes – but – before you go – I need you to listen
           to me – please don't ask why I'm about to give
           you the instructions that I am.

LORRY   Go on.

*CARTON goes to the rocking figure of MANETTE and checks his coat
pockets.*

He takes out a folded paper.

CARTON   We should look at this.

LORRY nods his consent.

CARTON opens it.

           Good.

LORRY   What is it?

CARTON   Wait.

CARTON takes out another paper from his own pocket.

             This is my Leave To Pass. You see –

LORRY holds it.

             Sydney Carton, a British man. Keep it for me
             'til tomorrow. Now take the Doctor's paper, it
             should allow him and Lucie and Little Lucie to
             pass the barrier, but I think it'll be annulled soon.

LORRY   Are they in danger?

CARTON   Barsad told me a wood-cutter, living by
             the prison wall, is under the control of the
             Defarges, and will say he witnessed Lucie
             making signals to prisoners. It threatens her
             life – and maybe the child's – and maybe even
             her father's. Don't look so horrified. You'll
             save them all.

LORRY   How?

CARTON   Pay for the quickest way of travelling to Calais
             tomorrow. Make sure the horses are ready to
             go at two o'clock in the afternoon.

LORRY   It'll be done.

CARTON   Tell her, tonight, of the danger that threatens
             her child and her father; and that for their
             sake she has to leave Paris. Tell her it was
             her husband's final arrangement. Make sure
             that all four of you are seated in the carriage,
             outside in the courtyard, at two. The moment
             I come to you, you drive away. Promise me
             that nothing will change your mind – or make
             you alter any details.

LORRY   Nothing.

CARTON   Any change – or delay – and lives will be lost.

LORRY   There won't be. I swear.

All light goes off except the light on DARNAY in his cell.
DARNAY finishes his letter. He seals it.

He lies down.

Blackout.

The guillotine falls. As it does so the lights come up suddenly and
DARNAY jolts up to sitting.

He paces around the cell with his arms folded in front of him.

Someone walks towards a microphone.

MIC   **Fifty-Two.**

Someone is entering the cell.

It is CARTON.

CARTON smiles and puts a cautionary finger to his lips.

CARTON   Of all the people on earth, did you expect to
                see me?

DARNAY   I can hardly believe it's you. You're – not –
                a prisoner?

CARTON   No. I have a hold on one of the gaolers here.
                I come from her – your wife – with a request.

DARNAY   Tell me.

CARTON   She – desperately – in the voice you love and
                remember –

DARNAY turns away – puts his hand to his eyes.

                – begs you to do as I say. I have no time to
                explain. Take off those boots and put on mine.

CARTON pushes DARNAY into a chair at the table.

Come on, do it!

DARNAY complies.

DARNAY	Carton – it's not possible to escape from here. You'll just die with me. / It's madness.
CARTON	I'm not asking you to escape. Change that cravat for this of mine – and our coats.
DARNAY	Carton! Don't add your death to mine.
CARTON	I have to ask you one thing – please answer me.
DARNAY	What is it?
CARTON	Manette's release from the Bastille – his being re-united with Lucie – that was you wasn't it? You made that happen.
DARNAY	Yes.
CARTON	Yes.
DARNAY	I'd appreciate it – if you kept that / to
CARTON	Of course. To the grave. You're a good man. You deserve everything. Write what I dictate. Quickly, please!

DARNEY picks up his pen.

CARTON has his hand by his chest and stands very close to DARNAY.

> Write exactly what I say. 'If you remember the things I said to you, a long time ago, you'll understand this when you see it. You do remember them, I know.'

CARTON is gently moving the hand near his chest, waving it near DARNAY's nose.

DARNAY looks at the hand and CARTON closes his fist tighter around something.

CARTON   Have you written 'I know'?

DARNAY   Yes.

DARNAY's eyes close.

                What's in your hand?

CARTON   You'll know very soon. Write! 'I am thankful
                that the time has come, when I can prove
                them. That I do so is no reason for regret or
                grief.'

The pen slips from DARNAY's fingers.

DARNAY   That smell......

DARNAY stands up suddenly and snatches towards CARTON's hand.

CARTON takes a step back and DARNAY staggers.

CARTON moves in quickly and holds a cloth to DARNAY's face.

DARNAY faintly struggles and then passes out.

CARTON quickly puts on the clothes DARNAY has taken off.

He goes to the door.

                Barsad.

BARSAD comes in.

                You see? There's very little risk.

CARTON signs the letter.

BARSAD   I knew you could look like him. I've seen that
                before. That's not the risk. My risk is you not
                going through with it.

CARTON is putting the letter in DARNAY's pocket.

CARTON   I will.

BARSAD	They're expecting fifty-two for the guillotine today. If the number is right you'll be fine in those clothes. It is remarkable.
CARTON	Now, get help and take me to the coach.
BARSAD	You?
CARTON	Him, man! This meeting to say 'goodbye' has overwhelmed me. I passed out. Call for help.
BARSAD	You swear you won't betray me?
CARTON	You're wasting time. Call them!

BARSAD calls at the door.

BARSAD	Some help here – quickly.
CARTON	Take him to the courtyard I showed you, put him in the carriage, show him to Lorry, tell him to remember what I said last night, and his promise of last night, and to drive away!

Two gaolers enter.

GAOLER 1	Jesus – what's gone on here?
GAOLER 2	Was he so upset that his little friend is off for a shave?
BARSAD	Lift him!

The gaolers pick DARNAY up.

	It's nearly your time, Evremonde.
CARTON	I know. Please be careful of my friend.
BARSAD	Let's go.

They leave.

Someone walks towards a microphone.

MIC	**The Final Hour.**

As they leave there are two strikes of the clock's bell.

RED CAPS come in and take hold of CARTON.

Music.

CARTON is dragged down through the shipping containers.

He passes other prisoners also being pushed or dragged by gaolers.

They are being counted.

A young woman is pushed into line.

RED CAP   47 –

They count other prisoners.

       48, 49, 50, 51 –

GAOLER 1   Get in that line, Evremonde.

He is pushed into a line.

RED CAP   52.

Other prisoners – most of whom are silent and still and looking at the ground.

The young woman, number 47, looks to CARTON.

Music still playing.

SEAMST   Citizen Evremonde.

She takes hold of his hand.

       You remember me.

He just looks at her.

       I'm the seamstress.

She lets go of his hand. She's unsure.

       I was in the women's cell next to yours.

CARTON   Of course. Remind me what you were accused
          of?

SEAMST   Plots. Plotting. But – I don't know anyone or
          anything. Who would think of plotting with
          me? No one's ever taken any notice of me.

CARTON puts down his head and weeps.

She puts her head down too.

          I'm not afraid to die, Citizen Evremonde,
          but I've done nothing. I would die for the
          Republic, if it – which is going to do so much
          good for us poor – if it would gain anything by
          my death; but I don't know how that can be.
          I'm just…a no one.

He touches her face.

          I heard you were released. I hoped it was true?

CARTON   It was. But, I was taken again and condemned.

She holds his hand again.

SEAMST   Please can I ride with you? Can I keep hold of
          your hand?

She looks up at him. He nods and smiles.

She drops his hand and takes a step back.

          Are you dying for him?

CARTON   Yes. And for his wife and child.

A pause.

They look at each other. Neither knows what to do.

SEAMST   How can you be so brave? Please let me hold
          your hand.

CARTON   Yes. Hush now, sister. We'll hold hands to the
          very end.

Someone walks towards a microphone.

MIC   **The Knitting Done.**

The music is still playing.

MADAME DEFARGE walks down with CLÉMENCE and A JACQUES.

MADAME D   She'll be at home, waiting for the moment of
             his death. She'll be mourning and grieving.
             She'll be in a state of mind to criticise the
             justice of the Republic. So I'll go to her.

A JACQUES   You're an adorable woman.

CLÉMENCE   To be cherished.

She embraces MADAME DEFARGE.

MADAME D   Take my knitting. And have it ready for me in
             my usual seat.

CLÉMENCE   You won't be late.

MADAME D   I'll be there before if starts.

She begins to move off.

CLÉMENCE   You beautiful soul.

Elsewhere PROSS and JERRY appear.

The music is still playing.

PROSS   Jerry – my girls only left here ten minutes ago
             – if our carriage leaves from the same place as
             theirs – don't you think it'll look suspicious.

CRUNCHER   I think –

PROSS   I don't want to lead any dirty French
             coachman here who's working for those
             stinkin' Red Heads – please let my little
             darlin's get home to Britain – please – I can't
             think – can't make a plan! Can you?

CRUNCHER   Well if –

PROSS   If you were to go now and stop our carriage
             before it gets here and wait somewhere for me,
             wouldn't that be best?

CRUNCHER   I reckon it –

PROSS   Where could you wait for me?

CRUNCHER   Well –

PROSS   The cathedral door.

CRUNCHER   That's a –

PROSS   Go then. Do it.

He nods and starts to go.

*Elsewhere on the stage MADAME DEFARGE appears and stares at
them both.*

The music is still playing.

JERRY turns back and looks at PROSS.

CRUNCHER   I'm worried about leaving yer. We don't know
             what'll happen.

PROSS   Go!

He nods and turns and goes.

PROSS stands alone.

MADAME DEFARGE moves to her.

PROSS sees her.

The music stops.

*In the following MADAME DEFARGE speaks in **French** and PROSS
in English:*

MADAME D   **The wife of Evremonde; where is she?**

PROSS   From the way you look you might be the wife
               of Lucifer. But you'll never get the better of
               me.

MADAME D   **I'm on my way to where they reserve my
               chair and keep my knitting for me. As I
               passed I thought I'd pay my compliments
               to her.**

PROSS   I'll hold my own against you.

They do not take their eyes off each other.

MADAME D   **Go and tell her that I wish to see her.
               Do you hear?**

PROSS   You can stare as much as you like – you won't
               shake me.

MADAME D   **You fucking imbecile you fucking pig!
               I demand to see her.**

MADAME DEFARGE takes a step forward.

PROSS holds up her arm to halt her.

PROSS   I don't care about myself.

Her voice is breaking and tears roll down her face.

               But I know that the longer I keep you here,
               the better chance there is for my little girls.
               I'll rip out every hair from your head if you
               lay a finger on me!

MADAME D   *(Laughing.)* **Awww what's wrong, you poor
               soft bitch.**

She calls out.

               **Citizen Doctor! Wife of Evremonde.
               Child of Evremonde! Anyone other than
               this useless fucking fool.**

She suddenly stops and thinks.

Are they gone?

PROSS   You know now don't you?

MADAME D   **If they're not here they're gone.**

PROSS   Yes – they've gone.

MADAME D   **Those evil bitches.**

She turns to go.

PROSS quickly grabs her, pulls her back and then stands in the way of where MADAME DEFARGE wished to go.

PROSS   You're not leaving here as long as I can hold you.

MADAME D   **Move or I will tear you to pieces.**

She goes to push PROSS out of the way.

PROSS grabs MADAME DEFARGE around the waist.

They struggle.

MADAME DEFARGE rips at PROSS' hair and face.

PROSS won't let go.

Suddenly there is a loud gunshot.

MADAME DEFARGE is shocked and then goes limp in PROSS' arms.

PROSS lets her fall to the floor.

PROSS looks at the dead body in horror.

She puts her hands to her ears and shakes her head in confusion.

She calls out.

PROSS   Hello! Hello!

She puts her fingers in her ears and wiggles them.

        I don't hear anything. Hello! Hello!

She claps near her ears.

She falls to the floor and sobs.

Nothing.

She then stands suddenly.

My baby girl. My darling girl.

She runs away.

We become more aware of the modern environment onstage.

News reports from Radios. TVs flick on, also broadcasting news.

The reports are political. About elections. Immigration. Fear mongering. Marches. Policing. Refugee crises. Bombings.

Within the body of the reports we hear these phrases repeated:

> **It was the best of times,**
> **it was the worst of times,**
> **it was the age of wisdom,**
> **it was the age of foolishness,**
> **it was the epoch of belief,**
> **it was the epoch of incredulity,**
> **it was the season of Light,**
> **it was the season of Darkness,**
> **it was the spring of hope,**
> **it was the winter of despair,**
> **we had everything before us,**
> **we had nothing before of us.**

The music is playing again.

Someone walks towards a microphone.

MIC **Calais.**

LORRY, MANETTE, LUCIE, LITTLE LUCIE and the sleeping DARNAY arrive in a van. They all wear 21C clothing.

French and UK border police in relevant uniforms look over the vehicle and its passengers. A UK BORDER FORCE OFFICER opens the door of the van.

UKBFO   Who've we got here then? Papers!

LORRY hands all the papers over.

          Alexandre Manette. Doctor. French. Where's he?

LORRY points him out.

LORRY   The Doctor's not well. He's in a very confused state.

UKBFO   The fuckin' fever of the Revolution too much for 'im?

LORRY   Yes.

UKBFO   It cracks a lot of 'em. Lucie. His daughter. French.

LORRY   This is her.

UKBFO   Lucie Darnay?

LORRY   Yes.

UKBFO   Another Lucie, her child. British. This is her?

LORRY   Yes.

The UK BORDER POLICE OFFICER crouches down.

UKBFO   Kiss me, sweetheart.

LITTLE LUCIE looks at her mother who nods. LITTLE LUCIE kisses the UK BORDER POLICE OFFICER on his cheek.

          Good girl. You tired?

LITTLE L Yes.

UKBFO   Bet you are.

He stands.

                    Sydney Carton. Lawyer. British.

LORRY   He's lying here.

UKBFO   Oh, yeah? Is he sick as well?

LORRY   Yes. He's not in good / health, generally.

UKBFO   Fuckin'ell – unbelievable.

LORRY   But – he's just separated from a friend – who –
            was about to be executed and – well it's / taken

UKBFO   Yeah yeah. I've heard it. Same story from all
            of you. Who doesn't know someone who's
            been executed or murdered or lost their
            parents. Everyone here's got the same story
            about how fuckin' dangerous it is – how hard it
            is where they've come from. Boo fuckin' hoo.
            Jarvis Lorry. Banker. British. That you?

LORRY   That's me.

UKBFO   Right then, Jarvis Lorry. That's it. You're
            done.

LORRY   Thank you.

THE UK BORDER FORCE OFFICER steps back.

LUCIE   Thank, God. Thank you, God.

LORRY   Ssshhhh.

They are heading towards the van.

The UK BORDER POLICE OFFICER steps towards them again.

UKBFO   Oy! Wait! Stop. What you all doin'?

LUCIE   You said we could go.

UKBFO   Not back in there – I just meant I'd finished
            with you. British over there –

He indicates to one area.

> French over there.

He indicates to another area.

> And he'll want to speak to you.

A FRENCH BORDER POLICE OFFICER is approaching them.

LUCIE   What – you can't split us / up

She sweeps her daughter up.

UKBFO   Put her down.

The FRENCH BORDER POLICE OFFICER speaks in French.

FBPO   **Are you French? Only French citizens in this zone.**

LUCIE   **No – no – this isn't fair –** this / is madness.

UKBFO   The woman is, the / kid's not.

LORRY   Surely you don't need to split them up.

UKBFO   The old / guy's French.

LUCIE   **You have to let me stay with my daughter –** you have to.

The FRENCH BORDER POLICE GUARD is pushing MANETTE towards his daughter. MANETTE clutches on his daughter's sleeve as she still carries LITTLE LUCIE.

FBPO   **Put the girl down.**

UKBFO   Give her to me.

He pulls the child away from LUCIE as the FRENCH BORDER POLICE OFFICER holds LUCIE back.

LITTLE L   *(Screaming.)* Mamma – Mamma!

LUCIE   Lucie! Please. **I'm begging you, please!**

He carries her over to the Britain area. LORRY, now in the Britain area picks up the little girl and shouts across to LUCIE.

LORRY   I've got her – it'll be / all right this is just procedure I'm sure.

The UK BORDER POLICE OFFICER pulls DARNAY out of the van and drags him the few yards to the Britain area.

FBPO   **I need to see your papers.**

LUCIE   **He has them.**

She points to LORRY.

         He has all our papers – we are travelling together we're a family. Charles. Please don't / hurt him!

LORRY   Shut up, Lucie. Stop it!

LUCIE   We just want to get out of here – we just want to get to Britain.

UKBFO   Yeah – everyone wants to get to fuckin' Britain, mate.

LUCIE   We're a family. That's my daughter – why are you doing this to us? Please – we just want to get to Britain. We just want to be safe.

Someone walks towards a microphone.

MIC   **The Footsteps Die Out For Ever.**

We are at the guillotine. A crowd awaits. They are all in 21C clothing.

CLÉMENCE rises from her seat. An empty seat beside her.

CLÉMENCE   Thérèse!

She looks around her.

         THÉRÈSE!

Has anyone seen her? Thérèse Defarge?

A WOMAN   She never misses. She's never late.

CLÈMENCE   THÉRÈSE!

The guillotine falls and there is a huge cheer.

The car is pushed slowly across the stage. The top is adapted so people can stand on top as though in a tumbril.

CARTON and the SEAMSTRESS are stood in it. They are holding hands. They and everyone else in the tumbril are in 21C clothes. There are three others in with them. One has her hands over her eyes. One sits, his head bowed. One does a disturbing dance, he sings too, drunk on the horror.

The guillotine falls and there is a huge cheer.

BARSAD is watching. He is biting his hand.

A head is held up and there is a huge cheer.

Music.

All we should hear from this point is the music, the crash of the guillotine, and the dialogue of CARTON and the SEAMSTRESS.

The dancing man is pulled from the tumbril and pushed towards the guillotine.

CARTON turns the SEAMSTRESS so her back leans in to his chest. He is between her and the guillotine.

SEAMST   Thank you. If it wasn't for you I wouldn't have
            found the strength to think of God and Christ
            who was put to death so that we might have
            some hope and comfort here today. I think
            you were sent to me by Heaven.

CARTON   I'm grateful that you're with me.

The guillotine falls.

The SEAMSTRESS starts. CARTON turns her face to his.

A head is held up.

> Keep your eyes on me. Nothing else.

The woman with her hands over her eyes is pulled from the tumbril and pushed towards the guillotine.

SEAMST   I don't mind anything while I hold your hand.
         And I won't mind anything when I let it go,
         if they're quick.

CARTON   They will be quick.

SEAMST   There's so much that I don't know. I feel
         stupid; but can I ask you something?

The guillotine falls.

CARTON   Of course. What is it?

SEAMST   My cousin is an orphan like me –

A head is held up.

> – we went to different towns to find work and
> she has no idea what has happened to me.

The seated man is pulled from the tumbril and pushed towards the guillotine.

> If the Republic really does good for the poor
> – and they become less hungry and suffer less,
> she might live a long time.

CARTON   Yes, gentle sister.

The guillotine falls.

SEAMST   What I've been thinking – is – do you think
         that it will seem long to me, while I wait for
         her?

A head is held up.

CARTON   I don't know.

SEAMST   Please tell me that you do.

He takes her face in his hands.

CARTON   You won't have to wait. As there is no time
              there.

SEAMST   Thank you. Do you believe that or are you just
              comforting me?

CARTON puts his head down.

              Do you even believe in God?

He keeps his head down.

              It doesn't matter – I still get comfort from you
              – and by what I believe.

He looks up and holds her face again.

              Am I to kiss you now? Is the moment come?

CARTON   Yes.

She kisses him on the lips.

SEAMST   God bless your soul.

He kisses her on the lips.

CARTON   Your God will bless you.

She is pulled from the tumbril and taken towards the guillotine.

Music still.

CARTON closes his eyes.

He waits.

The guillotine falls.

CARTON opens his eyes and looks at us.

I see their lives

I see the lives for which I give my life

I see them peaceful

I see them useful

I see them prosperous

I see them happy

I see the chance that Britain offers them

I see compassion

I see what we can be

I see our shared dreams

I see hope

I see love

I see Lucie

I see her with a child held close to her

I see the child has my name

I see that they hold me in their hearts

I see Lucie

I see her – an old woman now – crying for me
on the anniversary of this day

I see that child who has my name

I see him as a man bringing a boy also with my
name, to this place

I see this place, which then has not a trace of
this day's horror

I see that child

I see that future

Yes

It is a far, far better thing that I do, than I have ever done.

The guillotine falls.

Blackout.

The end.